LIFE IN TH

LIFE IN THE FAST LANE

Alain Prost

with Jean-Louis Moncet

*Translated from the French
by Edward John Crockett*

Stanley Paul
London Sydney Auckland Johannesburg

For my brother Daniel

Stanley Paul and Co. Ltd

An imprint of the Random Century Group

Random Century House, 20 Vauxhall Bridge Road,
London SW1V 2SA

Random Century Australia (Pty) Ltd
20 Alfred Street, Milsons Point, Sydney, NSW 2061

Random Century New Zealand Ltd
191 Archers Road, PO Box 40-086, Glenfield, Auckland 10

Century Hutchinson South Africa (Pty) Ltd
PO Box 337, Bergvlei 2012, South Africa

First published in French in 1988
by Editions Michel Lafon
First published in English in 1989
by Stanley Paul and Co. Ltd
Copyright © 1988 Editions Michel Lafon Paris
English edition Copyright © Stanley Paul, 1989, 1990

Set in Erhardt by ⚡ Tek Art Ltd, Croydon, Surrey

Printed and bound in Great Britain by Butler & Tanner

Cataloguing in Publication Data
Prost, Alain
  My Way.
  1. Racing cars. Racing. Biographies
  I. Title
  769.7′2′0924

ISBN 0 09 174471 7

Contents

    Acknowledgements 6
1 Racing – a second love   9
2 Karting crazy   15
3 Back to school   22
4 A demonstration of potential   26
5 A taste of reality   30
6 Moving through the gears   32
7 Enter McLaren   38
8 My first Grand Prix win   47
9 Twelve months too long   53
10 Pipped by Piquet   59
11 Farewell to Renault   64
12 Teaming up with a legend   68
13 Meet the crew   70
14 A successful Formula   74
15 The long road to the top prize   81
16 Friendship and rivalry   97
17 All change at McLaren   114
18 Senna's arrival   131
19 Putting my foot down   140
20 Image and fame   154
21 Champion again   156
    For the Record: 1973–1989   165
    Index   185

Acknowledgements

Thanks are due to the following, whose help and encouragement made this book possible: Anne-Marie Prost, André Prost, Marie-Rose Prost, Aram Djabourian, Dominique Faget, J.C. Francolon, Alain Lassale, Francis Apestéguy, Alain Denize, Bénédicte Pellerin, Pierre Marchetti, Patrick Boutroux, Pat Behar, Jacques Cochin, Régis Bulot, Jean Berchon, Gilles Levent, Bernard Derenne, Daniel Janin, Mansour Ojjeh, Guy Savoy and DPPI, G. de Keerle, Photothèque Renault, Oreca, Hugues Trevennec and Nigel Roebuck.

The following companies offered invaluable assistance at one stage or other in the preparation of this book: Pole Promotion, Patt, Air France, Rodoz SA, Pouilloux Moët et Chandon, Kodak, Nikon, Marlboro Press Service.

Special thanks are also due to the management and staff of the Gamma Agency for their patience and understanding.

The majority of photographs were supplied by Alain Prost's personal photographer, Bernard Bakalian. Others are courtesy of AllSport/Vandystadt; Stefan Johansson; Colorsport/Sipa Sport; Mark Newcombe; Nigel Snowden; Keith Sutton; Steve Yarnell; and Zooom.

The authors – Jean-Louis Moncet and Alain Prost

Bernard Bakalian, who took many of the photographs in this book, seen here with Jackie Stewart and Alain Prost

A picture of innocence: the Grand Prix driver as a child

1 *Racing – a second love*

My roots are in the *département* of the Loire, a rugged region in the heart of France which takes its name from the river that runs through it. The inhabitants of the region tend to be uncomplicated, outspoken and hard-working.

Even some of my best friends – such as Ron Dennis, the current boss at McLaren – habitually call me tight-fisted and intractable in my business dealings. And I suppose it is just feasible that there is some correlation between those traits (some would say defects) and my roots in that rather cold, austere area in and around Saint Etienne, Firminy and Saint Chamond: respectable, unprepossessing towns dominated by collieries, textile plants and steelworks.

Perhaps so. But I can't help wondering if my Armenian ancestors on my mother's side of the family might not have something to say about it.

I tend to be outspoken, even abrupt, but that's the way I am. I have always told the truth – at all costs and irrespective of the consequences. And, God knows, there have been and still are occasions when I could bite my own tongue off. I don't always react to all the demands made of me and on my time, and I don't always jump when people tell me to jump.

The simple fact is that I loathe being expected to project a world champion image – whatever that is supposed to be – or being paraded as some kind of ideal. I am simply not built that way: I choose my own line and I stick to it through thick and thin, in public and in private, on the track and off it. For me, the only genuinely important thing is to be honest with myself. Again, it is just feasible that this has something to do with how and where I was brought up.

I was born on 24 February, 1955 in Lorette, a township of 5000 inhabitants just outside Saint Chamond. A small family – my father

André, my mother Marie-Rose, and my brother Daniel, a good few years older than myself. Our house was in Rue Dugas-Montbel in Saint Chamond, and my father had a basement workshop there where he made tubes and piping and manufactured, among other things, kitchen furniture.

My childhood was happy and uncomplicated. I was like all the other kids on the street, neither better nor worse off than they were. Slightly spoilt perhaps, but no more so than the next. I had the same ups and downs, the same hobbies, the same anxieties, the same fads, fantasies and frustrations.

With the best will in the world, nothing in my childhood and upbringing could remotely be construed as an early indication of my later taste for speed and risk. By the same token, there was nothing in my family background that even hinted at my subsequent preoccupation with motor racing.

Years later, when I had started to win a race or two, my grandmother – a strong-willed, capable lady if ever there was one – remarked that, if I was so enthusiastic about working with cars, I would do better to open a gas station. For her, sport was most definitely *not* a serious profession.

Below left: *Never afraid of hard work – even at an early age*

Below right: *My grandmother, a strong-willed lady. She wanted me to learn a real trade (or so she said, the day I told her I was going to be a racing driver)*

It may not look that way, but I really loved soccer . . .

A great little team. I am kneeling in the front row, third from the right.
I usually played on the right wing

Even in my early teens, when I was old enough to start getting into all sorts of trouble, I had no interest whatsoever in things mechanical. Actually, it was always Daniel who would climb into the family car and star fiddling with the various knobs, switches and levers, yanking the steering-wheel in every direction, clearly driving a final triumphant lap towards an imaginary chequered flag. When I come to think of it, it was also Daniel who covered the walls of his room with photographs of the leading drivers of the day and, later on, with posters of Jim Clark or Jackie Stewart.

As for me, I preferred ball games, especially soccer. While Daniel was driving to victory at Le Mans, Silverstone and Hockenheim, I was out in the yard at 21 Rue Dugas-Montbel scoring the winning goal at Colombes, Wembley and Maracana.

It is perhaps not very surprising, therefore, that when I reached the age of consent I had great difficulty persuading the members of my family that I could make it in motor racing. One fine day, after I had won the title of *Pilote Elf* and when I was the reigning French champion in Formula Renault, I was allowed to take the wheel of the family saloon to drive my mother into Lyon. I suppose I must

FÉDÉRATION FRANÇAISE DE FOOTBALL

LICENCE JUNIOR | **1972-73**

Né du 1er août 1954 au 31 juillet 1956

Ligue Régionale du LYONNAIS

Nom du Club CL. OL. SAINT-CHAMONAIS

Nom PROST (en lettres majuscules) Prénoms Alain

Né le 24 février 1955 à LORETTE (LOIRE)

Adresse (résidence effective) 22 rue Duges Montbel St-CHAMOND

Indications obligatoires même s'il y a dissolution des Clubs ci-contre

Club de la précédente saison Néant

Dernier Club quitté ____ Saison ____

S'il s'agit d'un renouvellement, l'indiquer

Signature du Joueur : | Le Secrétaire Général de la Ligue :

RÉSERVÉ A LA LIGUE

A document I am very proud of: my football licence for Club Olympique Saint-Chamonais Juniors

have been driving a bit on the fast side and cutting the occasional corner. My mother was not amused: 'Slow down, be careful, slow down, not so fast, watch out . . .' Ultimately, I had no choice: she instructed me to pull up, and she took over. I was only eighteen, after all, so I had to do as I was told.

I loved soccer and I still follow European league games and go to matches whenever possible. When I was fifteen years old, I could spend days on end kicking a ball about. Then, as now, I have a deep need to exert myself physically. Sitting down at home with a book is anathema to me – I have to be on the move, I have to be doing something. I am off like a shot the moment someone suggests a round of golf or a game of tennis, but golf and soccer are the only two sports I can watch on television without getting fidgety.

I played a lot of soccer in my younger days, all the way through primary school and into my first years at the *lycée*. I devoured newspaper reports on local, national and international matches. I played schoolboy soccer at Saint Chamond, Saint Etienne and even Lyon, and it was a treat to go to those same grounds as a spectator and watch the professionals play.

My passion for soccer helped me in grammar school, because I needed to do relatively well at my studies if I were to fulfill my ambition to qualify as a gym instructor. I should add that I wasn't much of a scholar, however, although I was fair at modern languages. Since then, of course, Formula One has helped me acquire fluent English and Italian.

My first years in Formula One coincided with the halcyon days of Saint Etienne – *les Verts* – at national and international level. It so happened that Christian Lopez, one of the stalwarts of the 'Greens' in those days, was also keen on motor racing. One thing led to another, and I soon had a place reserved for me on the bench at Saint Etienne. The team has since gone through the occasional bad patch, but I am a loyal supporter to this day. And nothing gives me greater pleasure than when someone brings me in a Sunday paper a few hours before a Grand Prix, so that I can read up on all the French League results of the previous day.

When I was driving for Renault, the management told me that they would like to give me a present of some kind, but they were not sure what I might like. We were in Brazil and it was the eve of the Brazilian Grand Prix. You can imagine their astonishment when I said, fine, get me tickets for the Maracana.

They were as good as their word and, that Friday evening, Jacques Laffite, Michel Denisot, Johnny Rives, Jean-Louis Moncet and I were sitting in the soccer Mecca of South America watching a fabulous game between Flamingo and America, two of the top teams in Rio. It was fascinating to see first-hand the completely different brand of football peculiar to Latin America which has contributed so much over the years to the colour and spectacle of the World Cup.

I had come a long way from my modest beginnings in Saint Chamond where I played my little heart out on the right wing for the local *Club Olympique Saint-Chamonais*. I remember coming back injured from a match one day in 1967. That was enough for my mother. She declared that she had gone off soccer – it was far too dangerous a sport. Little did she know . . . .

2 *Karting crazy*

My father was a calm, easy-going, quiet, understanding man. One day, in the summer of 1970, he unwittingly did something that changed my whole life.

He had taken the whole family down to a small holiday home he owned near Cannes on the Côte d'Azur. After a few days of messing around in the water and on the beach, I was starting to get bored. Sensing that I needed a change of pace, my father took me to the Siesta, by night a celebrated discotheque on the coast road between Antibes and Cannes and, by day, a superb adventure playground with its own beach, swimming pools, trampolines and funfair where, for a modest sum, you could sample the joys of karting.

I took to the karts immediately – they had a special aura about them that somehow caught my imagination – and I couldn't wait to get behind the wheel of one. I had never driven before, but those first few laps went off without a hitch – not bad, when you consider that I had my arm in plaster at the time.

To the casual onlooker, nothing out of the ordinary had happened. Like a lot of other holidaymakers, I had spent part of a beautiful summer day at a funfair and done a few laps in a kart. That's all there was to it.

But I had just discovered a whole new world.

I wouldn't go so far as to say that I developed an instant obsession with things mechanical (if I did, I certainly wasn't conscious of it at the time), but I had made contact with something that appealed to me enormously – a curious amalgam of action, movement, violence, noise, smell, skill and imagination that bore a certain resemblance to a motor car.

At the time, I didn't try to analyse all this, but I knew one thing for certain: those few minutes on the track had been magic. Somehow, out there, you could express yourself, you could let your instincts take over, you could compete.

Left: *My father, a major force in my life, who introduced me to the pleasures of karting*

Below: *The good old days and soccer takes a back seat to life on four wheels . . .*

You could *live*.

Whatever it was – for the sake of argument, let's call it an obsession – I was so fascinated by the experience that, as soon as we got back home from the Côte d'Azur, I asked around in the neighbourhood to find out where the nearest kart track was. There wasn't one at Saint Chamond, but I was in luck a few kilometres farther away, at Rive de Giers. I signed up on the spot.

As a prelude to all this, I had been obliged to do a deal with my parents. In exchange for carrying on with my studies at the *lycée*, I could devote my evenings and weekends to karting. And to auto mechanics, because my preoccupation with kart racing had by now kindled an interest in engines and everything to do with them. (I remember once driving from Saint Chamond to the Nürburgring and back on a mini-scooter just to watch some big motorcycle event or other.)

As for the karts, I was completely hooked. No sooner had I joined the Rive de Gier Club than it dawned on me: I simply had to have my own machine.

All through 1971 I saved every last *centime* I could – it wasn't easy, I had to skimp on everything – until I had finally amassed the seven hundred francs needed to buy a second-hand engine and a second-hand chassis.

By 1972, I had a few good finishes to my name, enough to convince me that, just before the start of the 1973 season, I should take the plunge. I borrowed thirteen hundred francs – which, at the time, seemed to be an enormous amount – and bought myself a Vacquand chassis, in those days one of the best available.

From that moment on, financially speaking, I got by – more or less – on what I earned from kart racing. My total outlay had been all of two thousand francs. And it is a source of immense pride to me that, from that day to this, I haven't spent a single *centime* more on developing my career as a racing driver.

I drove to my first win with my Vacquand chassis. Other successes followed. I came second in the French championship behind another youngster who had already made a name for himself in kart racing, Jean-Louis Bousquet. I had my work cut out trying to keep up with Jean-Louis during my first few seasons in racing; although he was later to concentrate on his career as a lawyer, he still races production cars, and does so exceptionally well.

While I was competing in the French karting championships, I kept myself afloat by tuning engines and by playing poker, no doubt

Tool kit always at the ready

a less honourable pursuit, but nevertheless a distinctly more lucrative one, because I was an excellent player. My wins on the track were generating some valuable publicity and I used to spend my evenings in a little corner of my father's workshop tinkering with my own engines and those of a growing number of customers. Throughout, I received an enormous amount of encouragement and support from Claude Pelletier, the president of the Rive de Gier Club.

I was determined to compete in the 1973 world championships which were being held at the Nivelles track in Belgium. After a few mishaps along the way, I finished the race in fourteenth position – not brilliant by any means, but enough to win me an ardent fan who was later to become a friend and a key figure in the development of my career: Michel Fabre.

Michel owned a company called SOVAME, which imported the best karts on the market – Squale and Python chassis with Parilla and Komet engines. I struck a bargain with him: I would be his official dealer for the *départements* of central France, the Rhône and the Alps in exchange for his taking me on, so to speak, as a works driver.

This kind of arrangement was still comparatively rare in those days, but it helped me enormously. Above all, it enabled me to persuade my parents that I was now a fully-fledged professional. As a result, they gave me their official blessing to leave school. Round about this time, I also got to know Jannick Auxemery, who had left Formula Renault to concentrate exclusively on karting. Jannick really knew the ropes and he proved a great help to me.

1974 was a great year. I had wangled my way out of school one step ahead of the final form, I was racing on a regular basis and winning often.

I was also commuting between France and Germany (I had been called up for national service in November 1974 and was stationed in Trier) and every time I got back to Saint Chamond I would look up a pretty young blonde called Anne-Marie, who was something of a bookworm, who was training to be a teacher, and who was, at best, decidedly indifferent to the mysteries of karting. An added

With one of my team-mates, Michel Lesgourgues. At the time, I doubled as works driver and official distributor of SOVAME, the French importer of top-class karting equipment. The SOVAME line-up that year was Lesgourgues, Asselbur and Prost

My parents agreed to my leaving the lycée *to concentrate on karting. And my mother was one of my most loyal fans*

complication was that her parents didn't exactly view me as a young man with a rosy future. Nonetheless, I saw as much of Anne-Marie as I could . . . .

I won both the French championship and the European championship in 1974.

The 1974 world championship is still fresh in my mind. It was won by Riccardo Patrese, with Eddie Cheever in second place. Those two were among the stalwarts of Formula One at the time. Jean-Louis Bousquet was seventh, Beppe Gabbiani tenth, Piero Necchi sixteenth and Henri Toivonen eighteenth – all of them familiar figures, if not necessarily household names, in the autosport world of the 1980s.

Just recently, in an interview in *Karting International*, Eddie Cheever reminisced about his karting days and recalled – quite wittily – our regular duels during that marvellous period: 'I seem to remember a little guy with a broken nose. I couldn't get past him although I was faster than he was. I finally took him on the last lap. And he's made me suffer for it ever since . . .' Typically Eddie!

A few months later, I was one of the hot favourites for the 1975 Alazar Trophy which would feature the *crème de la crème* of the world's karting fraternity. I drove an impeccable race, putting a spanner in the works of a certain gentleman (whose name doesn't even deserve a mention in these pages) who held a monopoly on championship titles. One of his drivers deliberately forced me off the track and any chances I had of winning evaporated. I have always detested poor sportsmanship.

Immediately I crossed the line, I went straight over to the character who had rigged the race – all six foot plus of him – and punched him on the jaw. My licence was withdrawn for six months.

So, all I had to show for my efforts in the Alazar Trophy was a six-month suspension, which I duly sat out. Still, that didn't prevent me from winning another national title in 1975 – and that was a really important one in terms of my subsequent career.

Up to the early 1970s, the accepted way into motor racing had been via driving schools and then up through the various categories. However, one obvious fact gradually came to be acknowledged, namely that karting had played an important part in the success of several top names in Formula One – Emerson Fittipaldi, for one, Ronnie Peterson, for another.

The powers-that-be in French karting thus took an excellent decision when they started awarding scholarships to the most deserving kart drivers to enable them to go through driving school. I was one of the chosen.

On being awarded a scholarship, I opted to attend the Renault-Elf Winfield School at the Paul Ricard circuit. Kart racing had given me an opportunity to get to know a bit about autosport and it had become increasingly attractive. At the time, I hadn't mapped out any particular career plan, but moving on from karting and into formula racing seemed to be a logical step in the pursuit of my obsession.

I had turned a new page in my life.

3 *Back to school*

Once I had identified motor racing as a logical extension of karting, I started to devour autosport journals and reviews. At the time, every single one of them was praising a new circuit which had been built in Le Castellet in south-eastern France between Toulon and Marseille. It appeared that the new circuit was modern, safe and, because it was on the Côte d'Azur, almost always bathed in sunshine.

The circuit was called Paul Ricard. And the Winfield school, which had been set up next to the Magny-Cours circuit near Nevers, had now opened a second driving school there, backed by Renault and Elf.

The easy option would have been to attend Magny-Cours, which was much closer to Saint Chamond than Le Castellet. However, I was all too familiar with the vagaries of our local weather and the near-inevitability of rain. In the end, it had to be Paul Ricard.

My new school was a small room complete with blackboard – just like any traditional classroom, a 2·2 kilometre circuit which formed part of the 5·8 kilometre Paul Ricard circuit proper and which was accessed by a slip road, and a workshop/garage with cute little Martini single-seaters.

The instructors were characters in their own right and I have kept up my friendship with them to this day, although I must admit that I was not the easiest of pupils. Simon de Lautour was an engaging Brit and a connoisseur of the delights of the South of France. And Antoine Rafaelli was quintessential *Midi*.

My arrival at the Winfield school did not create any indelible impression. Today, they look back on me as the retiring young lad with the close-cropped hair who drove in from Trier in a clapped-out Renault 16.

I diligently followed the course. First, the theory, blackboard-style, then practice behind the wheel of a Martini. The instruction was decidedly classic; heel-and-toe acceleration and braking, exhaustive analysis of every corner, then a whole series of laps at predetermined revs – 3500, 4000, 4500, 5000, 5500 and, finally, 6000 rpm. Each pupil was timed for each series and the fastest went through to semi-finals and a final round, when only five were left.

I was a good learner, but I didn't really stand out from the rest and I didn't achieve particular distinction. This was in sharp contrast to previous pupils who had come out top at Winfield – such as Patrick Tambay who, four years before my time, had caught the eye of the instructors from the very first moment he took the wheel.

In fact, I didn't make any impression at all until we were lapping at 5500 rpm, which is to say, close to the rev limit.

Then it started to rain.

Rain is a fairly rare commodity at Paul Ricard, and, within no time at all, the trainees were spinning out right, left and centre. All except yours truly.

Antoine Rafaelli was on one side of the circuit and Simon de Lautour on the other. Both of them were dumbfounded. Simon jumped into his battered old van and raced over to Antoine. Both of them asked the same incredulous question: 'Did you see Prost?'

From that day on, I had the measure of the Martini and I became – to use Antoine's own terminology – 'a pain in the ass.' I earned this appellation for a very simple reason: once I was sure that I had the car where I wanted it, I began driving it like a kart.

Simon and Antoine had been doing their utmost to teach us the classic braking techniques of race driving – line the car up, hit the brakes firmly, ease off, go into the bend, then accelerate out of it. I was doing more or less the exact opposite, in typical karting style: hugging the nearside curve very early on and braking at the same time as the car started to drift outside.

Simon jumped on me time and time again – and in no uncertain terms. Because the cars had been set up for a distributed brake load appropriate to the technique we were being taught, I kept locking the nearside wheels and cornering in a spectacular cloud of smoke. The whole point of the lesson was that you don't brake as you start to drift. But, for me, the end result was all that counted.

Simon raved on and on, and Antoine kept showing him my lap times. They were both distinctly at a loss.

Then came examination time.

First of all, there were the semi-finals, which pooled the top twenty pupils of that year's intake. I had obviously made the cut. Ten of us were to be examined on the Saturday and the other ten on the Sunday. I was put into the Saturday group and we had strict

25 October 1975. I won the title of Pilote Elf *in this red* Martini

instructions to show up at eight o'clock on the dot, otherwise we would be held over to the following day.

I wasn't at all pleased about being assigned to the first group. I came late on Saturday morning with the trumped-up excuse (I subsequently came clean to both Simon and Antoine) that I had had a puncture on the way down.

Naturally, this white lie afforded me an ideal opportunity to check each individual car's performance under examination conditions and to pinpoint the one I would go for next day on the strength of its reliability· in terms of engine, brakes and overall performance. In short, the car that would guarantee me the best result. I decided on car number four. A red Martini.

Come Sunday morning, I was there on the stroke of eight. Antoine told me to go first. I promptly got into car number four, by far the best of the bunch, and qualified with ease for the final, which was scheduled for a few days later.

The final would decide who was to be awarded the title of *Pilote Elf,* a very useful distinction for anyone hoping to make his way in motor racing. The event was held before a jury of drivers and journalists, and the format called for the five finalists to drive the school circuit one after the other – three 'warm up laps', followed by five laps against the clock. Once all the times were in, the jury would go into a huddle and then announce the winner.

Each year, on the night before the final, Jeannette Chabot of the Elf press service used to interview the five finalists to put a kit together for the press. When she asked me the standard question, 'What will you do if you don't win the title?', I replied with all the aplomb I could muster: 'I will win it'. In her press dossier, Jeannette noted succinctly: 'Doesn't contemplate losing.'

The date was 25 October, 1975. I had already used up all my weekend passes, so I forged one – not difficult, to the extent that I had been assigned to the adjutant's office and had direct access to the appropriate rubber stamps.

Let's skip the details and get down to the important bits. I had forgotten to pack my all-in-one and Antoine Rafaelli lent me one of his. This time I had Martini number five. I beat the school circuit track record during warm-up. And I won. Next year, I would be a racing driver.

Some time later, I received a very friendly letter from the colonel commanding my regiment. He'd known all along about the forged pass, but, all the same, he congratulated me on my win and let it be known that there were no hard feelings.

4 *A demonstration of potential*

The title of *Pilote Elf* came complete with everything a fledgling race driver could hope for: a Formula Renault *monoposto* and enough funds to race it for a full French championship season.

Elf bought me a Martini MK17 and my engines were entrusted to Bernard Mangé, who answers to the nickname 'Nanar'. He was already one of the best engine men in France and, to this day, he is still at the top when it comes to technical expertise and engine preparation. We set up shop in Magny-Cours along with my mechanic Jean-Pierre Nicolas.

My life as a racing driver began as I had always imagined it would. It was a nomadic life, travelling between circuits, making new friends, taking the good times with the bad.

I found the 1976 season genuinely easy. I won every race. Well, all but one.

The Formula Renault season called for thirteen races. I won the first twelve and I was already French champion before the final race, which was scheduled for the Imola circuit in Italy. There, ignition trouble – or maybe it was something to do with the fuel feed – prevented me from driving a good race.

Renault and Elf had sent out invitations to a party to celebrate the end of the Formula Renault season, and I was showered with congratulations as the new champion. Unfortunately, I had just lost a race and I tended to shrug off the well-wishers, because I was furious at having been so close to the grand slam I so dearly wanted.

I haven't changed all that much to this day. When I hold all the trumps, I hate losing. You may recollect how it was in the 1988 Hungarian Grand Prix. I was fastest man on the circuit throughout every phase of the race. A miniscule technical hitch made all the difference and I would have been beside myself with rage if several years' experience hadn't taught me a modicum of self-control.

Anyway, there it was: I had won twelve out of the thirteen races on the 1976 Formula Renault calendar. And I had posted eleven pole positions and eleven fastest laps. Despite all that, my most vivid recollection of that year is not of victory but of defeat.

In 1975, Renault introduced Formula Renault Europe, which ran parallel to Formula Renault proper. The Formula Renault Europe cars were more powerful, with wider tyres, and they outperformed those in the regular Formula Renault category. Not surprisingly, most of the better drivers who had preceded me in 1975 had moved

My Formula Renault machine was a real beauty. I won twelve races out of thirteen in this Martini

I won several Formula Renault races in 1976 before being invited to try out twice in the next category up, Formula Renault Europe. Here I am in a Danielson team Lola

up in 1976 and were competing in Formula Renault Europe, among them Didier Pironi, Jean-Louis Bousquet, Danny Snobeck, Marc Sourd, Alain Cudini and Richard Dallest.

I had already notched up three wins in Formula Renault in 1976 when Jacques Brussel, who ran the Danielson team with Dallest and Cudini in the Lola, suggested that I try out alongside them in the Formula Europe category. The race was to be run in Dijon. I had absolutely no hesitation about accepting his offer.

I started off by posting the fastest time in training. Next day, I had the fastest time in the qualifying laps, which put me in pole position for my qualifying heat. I won it ahead of Snobeck, Ethuin and Debias. Didier Pironi had won the other qualifying heat, and we shared the first row of the grid as the final got under way.

I have no idea what trivial mechanical problem stopped me getting away to a good start. Whatever it was, I was stuck on the grid and the first few cars immediately behind me pulled out past me. At the end of the first lap I was lying back in ninth place. I knew that I would have to pull out all the stops if I was to make any sort of favourable impression.

I reeled them in one by one, making my way past Haran, Debias, Dallest, Ragnotti, Ethuin, Snobeck and Cudini. The next thing I knew, I was in Didier Pironi's slipstream. That is as far as I got: my engine started to belch smoke and I had to retire when it finally gave up the ghost. It turned out that Bernard Mangé hadn't had time to tighten down the cylinder head cover bolts and the oil had simply leaked away.

One race official had been all for putting seals on my engine because one of the other drivers had lodged a protest, no doubt because he felt that my performance could only be due to a non-regulation engine. He went to a lot of trouble for nothing. But that wasn't the first time or, for that matter, the last, that I have had to cope with a suspicious rival whose main problem was his own mediocrity. I didn't worry about it too much, nor about having had to retire prematurely. What was pleasing and more to the point was that I had given a clear demonstration of my potential.

I went quickly back to Formula Renault at the national level, where I still had nine races to win. A few weeks later, I again tried out in Formula Renault Europe, this time at Zolder in Belgium. But I got off to a poor start (yet again!) and somehow managed to spin out of the race.

Never mind, time was on my side.

5 *A taste of reality*

As national champion and Formula Renault title-holder, I was theoretically entitled to move up to Formula Renault Europe on a full-time basis. That I was able to do so in practice was thanks to François Guiter, the great patron of autosport at Elf.

The championship involved sixteen races, and most of the leading contenders from the previous season were back again, bristling with experience and ambition. I knew it would be a tough season, and it was. What is more, anticipating the struggle ahead, I had asked François Guiter if I could drive as an independent – in other words, if I could run my own outfit and handle my own budget rather than be integrated into a team. This is what Didier Pironi had done the previous season.

My first adversary was Danny Snobeck, who racked up four victories on the trot at the start of the season, including Le Mans, Hockenheim and Monaco. I came back at him by winning at Nogaro and Magny-Cours. Meanwhile, none other than Jean-Louis Bousquet had twice posted the fastest lap time – needless to say, the same Jean-Louis I had crossed swords with several times in the karts. Bousquet won at Pau, Zolder and Clermont-Ferrand. Then I took the honours at Rouen and, once again, at Nogaro. Enter Jacques Coulon, another force to be reckoned with, who spoilt the party for us by taking first place at Magny-Cours and at Paul Ricard.

There were only three races left. I duly won the first two of them – at Monza and in Albi. The last race of the season was on 16 October at Paul Ricard.

In the race for the title, I was leading Bousquet, who had turned out to be as consistent as myself. I had a few points in hand. To take the title, I had to finish in no worse than seventh position in the final race of the season.

From left to right: *Prost, Danny Snobeck, Jean-Louis Bousquet and Richard Dallest. They fought me every inch of the way, but it was to be my championship*

On the day, my engine was not at its best, although I did post the fastest lap time. Accordingly, when I was assured of seventh place, I held position and didn't push too hard. It was the smart thing to do. Bousquet finished first but, in the final championship standings, I pipped him by three points: he had 154 points and I had 157.

That season in Formula Renault Europe is still very vivid in my recollection, probably for two reasons. First of all, it had really been a struggle, both technically and physically. I had been forced to cope with pressures which, then, at least, seemed immense. The battle for the title had been fought out under very difficult conditions, and I had had to come to terms with the realities of the sport – a far cry from my first season in Formula Renault, when everything had seemed so pleasurable and simple. What is more, I had started to notice – from one or two casual comments and from one or two caustic exchanges with individuals said to be in positions of power within the sport in France – that success (in this case, my success) was not always wholeheartedly appreciated. If anything, however, all this did was to reinforce my determination to succeed.

31

6 *Moving through the gears*

Apart from winning the championship, my experience in Formula Renault Europe had been positive in another sense: it had introduced me to a certain number of circuits outside France.

However, I harboured no illusions – Formula Europe was a purely French affair and the drivers who took part didn't acquire an international reputation overnight. The same held true for Formula Ford in the United Kingdom and Formula Vee in Germany, as well as for their respective 'super' categories. These were highly similar to and no more cosmopolitan than Formula Renault Europe. The organisers, with every justification, had taken advantage of the slot left vacant by Formula Three, a genuinely international category that was wasting away because it was prohibitively expensive to run.

The international governing bodies took action to remedy this situation and restore Formula Three to its rightful technical and competitive status. In France, two men in particular were instrumental in the resuscitation of Formula Three – François Guiter and Hughes de Chaunac. The latter's racing service company ORECA represented the interests of Tico Martini, the constructor of French single-seater racing cars based in Magny-Cours.

I had to ask myself what I should do next. Should I stay another season in Formula Renault Europe – not a bad living, incidentally, because the prize money was quite substantial – or should I go for broke?

I chose to place my trust in Hughes, Tico and François Guiter. In much the same way as he had persuaded Renault to get into Formula Two and Formula One, using the V6-Renault Sport engine developed by François Castaing and Bernard Dudot, François Guiter had talked the management of Renault Sport into commissioning and constructing a Formula Three engine based on a Renault 20TS four-cylinder.

32

The plan was put into action, and the Renault engine was installed in a Formula Three Martini entrusted to ORECA. Thus, Hughes de Chaunac was my first team manager before becoming, as he is today, one of my closest friends.

That first 1978 season in Formula Three was long and difficult. The engine had to be developed as a genuine racing car engine, which is never easy. And I had to start following team orders and observing constructor specifications. I didn't take too kindly to this.

I took even less kindly to losing. By midway through the season – which wasn't going by quickly enough for my liking – I was thoroughly depressed.

At the end of the 1977 season, when I had still been racing in Formula Renault Europe, I had accepted an invitation from the Kauhsen team to drive one of its Formula Two cars at Nogaro and in Estoril. The car in question was an old Elf 2-Renault, not particularly competitive and, above all, badly set up. In fact, I came close to a serious shunt in Estoril when I lost a wheel and spun out.

What is more, Fred Opert's US stable had already offered me a Formula Two drive in a Chevron-Hart at the 1978 Grand Prix in Pau. With Elf's help, I had taken them up on the offer and driven the fifth-best qualifying time, although I had to retire from the race itself with a blown engine.

And here I was, stuck in Formula Three, bored to tears and asking myself if I hadn't made the wrong move after all. Wouldn't it perhaps have been smarter to look for a drive in a good Formula Two team?

As things turned out, however, we were beginning to make some headway in Formula Three and, all in all, the 1978 season taught me some very valuable lessons. Being involved with Hughes de Chaunac and the ORECA team opened my eyes to a lot of things that are absolutely essential if you want to function effectively as an international racing driver.

As I said, we were making headway: little by little, the Martini-Renault began to make its mark. At long last, I was beginning to get among the points – a fourth place in Monaco, a third at Silverstone, and a win at Jarama. I finished the season in ninth place in the European Championship and won the French Formula Three title.

Needless to say, as the 1979 season came closer, I was faced with exactly the same dilemma as before: should I stay in Formula

Three? My ultimate ambition was still to be in Formula One and I seriously assessed my chances of getting a drive in the highest category. I was young. And when you're young, there is a tendency to rush things. On the other hand, people looked upon me as a rational, stable sort of person. My big worry was that I might be too rational and too stable. If I spent too much time weighing the pros and cons, I might end up by missing a golden opportunity.

François Guiter knew the ins and outs of Formula One, particularly as far as its financial and technical requirements were concerned. He advised me to drive a second season in Formula Three.

I was still in two minds. I have always believed that, whatever happens, a racing driver's career should follow an exponential curve. That being the case, what about Formula Two? But that was a dead letter in France now that Renault and Elf had pulled out. As for Formula Three, my previous season had been moderate at best. Maybe a second season would be better? Then, again, maybe it would be worse . . . .

Clearly, I didn't know which way to jump. Deep down, I knew that François Guiter and Hughes de Chaunac were right. I knew it in my heart of hearts, but that still didn't stop me being furious with myself at the prospect of having to repeat a year. However, there was one small consideration that tipped the balance. Renault Sport had fully committed its resources to Formula Three, a clear indication of the total backing of the parent company Régie Renault, which had appointed Gérard Larrousse head of competition a few years previously.

In the event, Renault's commitment was well-founded. I had a superb season in European Formula Three Championship – and a lot of fun besides. I won at Zeltweg, Zolder, Magny-Cours, Zandvoort, Knutstorp, Jarama, la Châtre and Albi, taking both the French and European titles. And there was one other triumph, the most sought after of them all, namely a Formula Three victory at Monaco.

Under the leadership of Hughes de Chaunac, and with expert mechanics such as Robert Descombes and Fernand Lidouren (later to become team chief in top French stables such as Renault-Sport and Peugeot-Talbot Sport), the Martini-Renault had become a marvellously efficient machine. We had hit a winning streak, the team got along famously, and there was a real sense of *joie de vivre*. We were winning and we didn't have a care in the world.

Monaco, 1979: my finest victory in Formula Three

The Martini-Renault had problems in 1978 but the next season it started to perform really well

In Monaco, just a few hours before the race was due to start, the local police still had me under lock and key for some minor indiscretion or other. I gesticulated so wildly that I broke their switchboard and they reckoned it was probably more prudent to get rid of this whirling dervish as soon as possible. At Zandvoort in Holland, once again immediately before a race, Richard Dallest locked me out on the balcony of our hotel room, five floors up, and vanished. I had to batter down the glass door with the help of a chair and a few well-placed kicks. Those were the days!

Before going to Jarama, I detoured to Zandvoort to watch the Dutch Grand Prix – just to make sure that Formula One was managing to get along without me. When I arrived – the future Formula Three champion of Europe, no less – I was in for a shock. People were civil, but they couldn't have cared less who I was. François Guiter duly intervened on my behalf and introduced me to various Formula One supremos, but my only real contacts were with Fittipaldi and with McLaren, who weren't exactly in a position to lord it in those days.

I waited until I had the European Formula Three title safely tucked away before setting off on a trip to North America, together with my journalist friends Eric Bhat and Jean-Louis Moncet, to watch the final two Grand Prix races of the 1979 championship.

In Canada, Niki Lauda announced his retirement in spectacular fashion. Slap bang in the middle of practice, he gathered up his gear, went back to his hotel, and announced that he had called it a day. This left Brabham boss Bernie Ecclestone somewhat in the lurch and, eventually, it was the Argentinian driver Ricardo Zunino who stepped in at the last moment to drive the second Brabham alongside Nelson Piquet. At Watkins Glen, there was some talk of my taking over from Zunino in the Brabham. Teddy Mayer, who ran McLaren, repeated an offer he had made to me at Zandvoort. If I wanted to, I could be behind the wheel of a McLaren in the US Grand Prix.

It was obviously tempting, but I am cautious by nature, and I didn't want to prejudice my grand entry by chancing a one-off drive for which I was not fully prepared. I turned the offer down, but I asked Teddy Mayer to let me try out for him whenever was convenient once the season was over.

He agreed.

7 *Enter McLaren*

It was some time after the US Grand Prix and I had still heard nothing from Teddy Mayer.

I went through that period of nagging self-doubt which, as I now know, many drivers experience every season. This is when you have to show yourself a skilled negotiator, balancing your financial expectations against the drives that are available. The fact was that I didn't have a very strong negotiating position. I had some talent and a couple of titles under my belt, but I was a novice as far as Formula One was concerned.

Teddy hadn't forgotten me, however. He was in the process of releasing Patrick Tambay, and was planning to keep John Watson as his number one driver and bring in a young hopeful to fill the number two slot. Just to keep the pressure up, he let slip that another driver was in the running – Kevin Cogan, for whom Teddy's American contacts had the highest regard. At the time, Cogan was the big name in Formula Atlantic, the US equivalent of Formulas Three and Two.

On a beautiful day in November I finally took off for Paul Ricard to try out for Formula One. I sat in the cockpit as the mechanics adjusted the pedals to my height and I held a Formula One steering-wheel for the very first time. A dream come true.

I didn't give any thought to Cogan (who, incidentally, made a career for himself in Indycars). I knew he didn't stand an earthly chance against me and, as it turned out, I drove him into the ground.

After the try-out, where I proved to be the fastest, Teddy Mayer invited me over to England to sign a contract. I was in Formula One and I was pleased, but I wasn't over the moon. McLaren was far from being one of the top teams and I knew I was in for a rough ride in the season ahead.

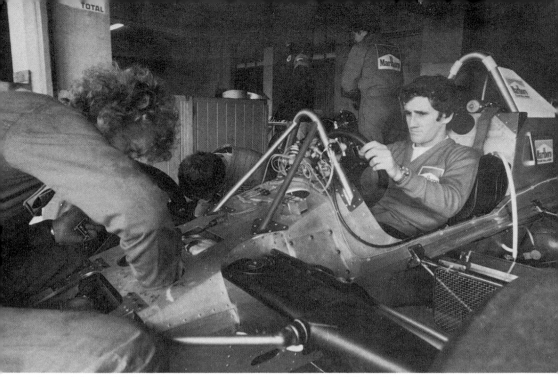

One of the highlights of my career: with McLaren at Paul Ricard, my first moments behind the wheel of a Formula One car

What it came down to was that I had to make my presence felt in a marque that was really among the also-rans. And I had to do so at every conceivable opportunity. On the other hand, there was a very positive aspect to my contract with McLaren. I was joining the Marlboro clan, which had been pumping money into Formula One for several years.

All in all, things seemed to be moving in the right direction. I had started out four years previously in Formula Renault and my progress had been rapid, although by no means as spectacular as that of an Emerson Fittipaldi, Jacky Ickx or Elio de Angelis.

My first Formula One Grand Prix season opened on 13 January 1980 on the Almirante Brown circuit in Buenos Aires. It was high summer in the southern hemisphere and the cockpit temperatures were unbearable. Worse still, you could actually see the asphalt starting to melt. The circuit had been patched and re-patched – all to no avail. After practice, the foundation blocks of the circuit were showing through, particularly in the corners, where wear-and-tear was at its most pronounced.

I vividly recall a painful scene during the pre-race briefing. Fangio – the great Juan Manuel Fangio, for me a living legend – suggested, although perhaps not in so many words, that we make a special effort to keep our speed down in the early laps. Keep our speed *down*? That was the great Fangio's advice to Formula One drivers who were dedicated to doing precisely the opposite? I was completely stunned. Of course, I realise now that Fangio had no option – he was acutely embarrassed at the state of the circuit, but obliged to be a diplomat in his own country.

Driving on a circuit that is breaking up is like driving on packed ice. The tyres don't grip, they slip and slide. As a result, that Argentinian Grand Prix was pure Russian roulette. As I said earlier, I knew that I had to take every opportunity to make my presence felt in my first season. This was just such an opportunity. I couldn't compete on an equal footing with crack teams like Williams, Ligier, Renault, Ferrari and Brabham; and I realised that their drivers were much more experienced than myself. But I also knew that, on a surface like this, the race would be long and full of incident. My race plan was simple: drive as prudently as possible.

That's exactly what I did. I admit that I went into a double spin at one point during the race, but I doubt very much if anyone remembers it, especially when you take into account how many other incidents there were and how many drivers retired. I came sixth out of seven finishers and notched up my first point in a Formula One world championship.

I'd made the most of my very first opportunity to make people sit up and take notice. I had dinner that evening with the small group of French journalists who had decided to take me under their wing. I was the new boy and I didn't belong with the in-crowd led by hell-raisers like Jacques Laffite, Jean-Pierre Jabouille or Jody Scheckter. Still, I was delighted to have a chance to relive the day's events in the company of people who knew what they were talking about.

Two weeks after the Argentinian Grand Prix, we were in Brazil for the second race of the season. My approach was going to be very much the same as before. The Interlagos circuit is very difficult, very dangerous and very, very unpleasant because large sections of it are so unpredictably bumpy that there is no way of knowing how the car will react. This being the case, I knew that I had yet another opportunity to turn in a good performance.

Riccardo Patrese helped. Riccardo had been driving in Formula One since 1977 and, although he was still looked upon as a

My mother has kept all my trophies – from the early karting days right through Formula One

beginner, he had already carved out a reputation as a no-holds-barred driver who was difficult to pass. There was an unusually vindictive streak in his nature and my more experienced colleagues warned me that he would use any means at his disposal – even the most reprehensible – to avoid being overtaken. Having said this, I hasten to add that he is now very much a reformed character and is today – at least, as far as I am concerned – a perfect gentleman on the track. As of lap twenty-six of the forty-lap 1980 Brazilian Grand Prix, however, Riccardo proved that he still had some way to go in this respect.

Immediately I came up behind him on lap twenty-six, Patrese tried every trick in the book – and quite a few that weren't – to block my McLaren. It took me *eleven* laps to pass his Arrows, but I eventually made it. It was worthwhile, because a fifth place in the Grand Prix was at stake.

I had picked up another two world championship points. I was congratulated on my performance in Brazil, not so much because of the points, but mainly because I had shown patience and skill in my duel with Patrese.

I genuinely felt I had achieved certain of my Formula One goals in the short space of fifteen days and I could hardly wait for the next race – the South African Grand Prix at Kyalami – to do even better.

McLaren had built a new car for the next stage of the championship. The new M29C was the original M29 with an entirely revamped front suspension. The big question was whether the new suspension had been accurately calibrated or whether it was too weak.

We soon had our answer. During practice, a piece of the front axle assembly sheared at the very instant I was coming into Leukoop, and I ploughed straight ahead and smashed into the wall. The main thing was that I came out of it unhurt – but not for long.

For the qualifying laps on the following day, it was back to the old M29B; this time, it was the rear axle assembly that folded as I went into the S-bends coming up to Leukoop. I hit the wall once more and fractured my left wrist. I was out of the South African Grand Prix and I was unable to start in the next race, the US Grand Prix West at Long Beach.

Despite Teddy Mayer's reassurances, these two shunts made me somewhat sceptical as to how good McLaren's mechanics really were. However, when you are a young driver setting out to make a name for yourself in Formula One, it isn't particularly advisable to make known your feelings along those lines. Only my closest friends guessed that all was perhaps not as it should be.

John Watson, the number one driver in the McLaren team at the time, was extremely supportive after these two incidents. I had – and still have – a great affection for John. He was always on hand with helpful advice, he knew the circuits backwards, and he never failed to pass on a couple of pointers if I didn't happen to be familiar with the ideal line on some circuit or other.

John was under no obligation to be so helpful and forthcoming – God knows, I was beginning to make life difficult for him in all manner of ways. In all honesty, even at the risk of appearing boastful, I was better than John when it came to setting up the cars – and, as a result, I was faster. Clearly, the most immediate and most dangerous competitor in Formula One is your own team-mate: more often than not, he has exactly the same car as you and his performance is thus a yardstick against which to measure your own.

John himself was very much aware that he was in for a difficult season and it wasn't long before tongues started to wag. A couple of facetious remarks were made – not only by outsiders but even within the McLaren squad – and I was very upset by the whole thing. One of the team mechanics – a chap called Tony, nicknamed 'Teach' – drew a couple of cartoons which I didn't find at all funny. I told him as much and, in no time at all, my own original nickname of 'Tadpole' had been changed to 'Napoleon'. I am all for a sense of humour, but I have to say that, had I been in John's place, I wouldn't have put up with this particular brand.

The 1980 season kept going at this somewhat chaotic pace. After missing out on Long Beach, I came back for the Belgian Grand Prix, where I was out of the points. I retired two hundred metres after the start in Monaco after Derek Daly's Tyrrell took to the air in spectacular fashion and nearly landed right on top of me.

I still had my doubts about the prospects for Teddy Mayer and his team. And my worst fears were brutally confirmed during practice at the Spanish Grand Prix (which, by the way, didn't count towards the world championship due to a complete break between FISA, the autosport international governing body, and FOCA, the Formula One constructors' association).

Halfway through practice, I came off the track as a result of mechanical failure in a tight left-hander at the bottom of a very fast downhill straight. At the insistence of several drivers, especially

Jacques Laffite, a wide run-off zone had been added at exactly that point in the circuit – thank God – otherwise I would have been smashed against the 'safety' rail. I was unhurt. But, as I clambered out of the wreckage, I knew that serious damage had been done to my self-confidence.

At McLaren, there were all kinds of odd things that I could never quite get used to. From time to time, Teddy Mayer's thinking seemed to me to be fifty years out of date. A case in point was the Italian Grand Prix at Imola, when he got us out of bed at four-thirty in the morning to make sure we didn't get bogged down in race-day traffic. Sure enough, we were at the track by five a.m., and we had to wait a good three hours before we could even have breakfast. In circumstances like those, how on earth can you be expected to develop the concentration you need to drive a Grand Prix?

The highlight of the third part of the season was the introduction of a new McLaren, the M30. I was given the job of setting the car up, which, all things considered, was a clear indication of the confidence they now had in me.

The M30 was a better all-round performer than the M29, but it was dangerously fragile. The suspension packed in, as was its wont, during the Canadian Grand Prix. I spun out at Watkins Glen for

This McLaren was never in the running. It had one massive problem – reliability. My season was a chapter of mechanical failures, particularly due to suspension problems

Up among the big boys: all the French Formula One drivers turned up to drive in a special R5 event to celebrate the anniversary of the Magny-Cours circuit. From left to right: Jacques Laffite, Jean-Pierre Jarier, Jean-Pierre Jabouille, Patrick Depailler, Didier Pironi, yours truly and René Arnoux

precisely the same reason, the only difference being that, this time, I was knocked cold on impact and my wrist hurt like hell. I was whisked off to the first-aid tent and my spirits soon revived, but there were to be longer-term after-effects of that particular shunt, notably a fractional loss of vision in my left eye. I also had difficulty sleeping, which was bad news for Anne-Marie because, being me, I couldn't lie there and watch her snoozing peacefully.

I gave it another try during the warm-up on Sunday morning (after all, I had qualified), but I was not in good enough shape and I withdrew from the race. That was it. I'd had enough of McLaren. I picked up my odds and ends and left, slamming the door behind me.

My first season in Formula One had ended in divorce – and a stormy one it would prove to be. But the season hadn't been a total washout, far from it. First and foremost, I had begun to get to know what Grand Prix racing was all about. I now knew how to react to and interact with the Grand Prix world and those who were part and parcel of it – the professionals (i.e. the drivers), the technicians, the sleeping partners, the media, and the others, the troublemakers, the hangers-on and the bullshitters of every hue. I had also met some genuinely interesting people, some of them at McLaren, including John Watson and a shy new engineer called John Barnard.

As if the ups and downs in my professional life weren't enough, I had contrived to complicate matters even further in my private life. On 1 August 1980, I had married Anne-Marie, as young, pretty and blonde as ever, a sensible, alert, cultured young lady who was *still* indifferent to the charms of motor racing. Anne-Marie was anxious to pursue her own career as a nursery school teacher, and I bought her a Range Rover to negotiate the tough winter roads in the *Massif Central*. By this time, we had a modern apartment in the Rue Victor Hugo in Saint Chamond, complete with a study for myself. According to my friend Jean-Pierre Jabouille, I was starting to develop a serious case of telephonitis.

At long last, I had what most men have at one time or other in their lives: an intimation of mortality. Death tends to be an abstract concept or no more than a few column inches in a newspaper, until it strikes close to home. Patrick Depailler was not yet a close friend but, quite simply, he had been the first among the Formula One drivers to come up to me and offer a helping hand. Why, I don't know. Perhaps he thought that we were alike in many ways. Patrick was killed during a practice lap at Hockenheim on the same day I got married.

8 *My first Grand Prix win*

My confidence in McLaren had evaporated and, despite having signed a two-year contract, I accepted Gérard Larrousse's offer of a Renault Turbo and the number two spot to René Arnoux.

Jean-Pierre Jabouille had been the number one driver for Renault and had been involved since 1977 in the development of Renault Sport Formula One cars. But he had clashed with Larrousse during the 1980 Italian Grand Prix at Imola, accusing him of favouring Arnoux. Because of this, he was scheduled to join Jacques Laffite at Ligier for the 1981 championship season.

Contract time; I left McLaren to join Renault on the eve of the 1981 championship. From left to right: *Gérard Larrousse of Renault, my Formula One team-mate René Arnoux, and Jean Ragnotti, an excellent rally driver*

I had one hell of a time extricating myself from McLaren. Teddy Mayer pointed out in no uncertain terms that I had signed a two-year contract. He didn't seem to appreciate that there is no point in keeping a driver against his will. I had to appeal to Renault's legal department to pry me loose.

As it happened, Teddy Mayer had to break off the contest. Marlboro, which had acquired the major say in the McLaren organisation, was in the process or rebuilding the team by putting one of its own men in charge – Ron Dennis, who had cut his teeth on Formula Two. The perceived need to recast McLaren confirmed to me that my own misgivings had been well-founded.

The start of the season was slightly delayed, but it got under way with the US Grand Prix West at Long Beach in California. This Grand Prix was to put an end to the power struggle between FISA and FOCA (spearheaded by Brabham boss Bernie Ecclestone) which had dominated 1980 and the close season of 1980/81.

In a nutshell, the international autosport ruling body had demonstrated a remarkable degree of laxity over the previous few years to the point where, little by little, Formula One had developed as a state within a state. To reassert its authority, the federation had espoused a particularly powerful cause: the abolition of 'ground effect', the generic term used to describe an aerodynamic phenomenon produced, among other things, by skirts which sealed the inverted wing Formula One underbodies. The net effect was to develop cornering speeds that were absolutely horrendous and completely inconsistent with track safety. What is more, ground effect cars were not attractive to drive and the driver had increasingly less opportunity to show his paces. In a fast corner, ground effect literally pinned the car to the track, the result being that driving skill was virtually an irrelevance on even the most challenging circuits: all you had to do was point the car in the right direction, keep your foot to the floor and let the car drive itself through the corner.

At one point in the 1980/81 close season, FOCA was close to secession. Fortunately, however, the two sides contrived to reach some sort of agreement and, when the cars lined up at Long Beach in March 1981, the skirts had disappeared.

I have very vivid memories of that championship season, starting at Long Beach itself, where I managed to shed a rear wheel in qualifying by getting too close to a wall. That was a trifle embarrassing and I was in no hurry to get back to the pit lane.

48

Early days in the Renault-Turbo: a brush with the walls at Long Beach

Instead, I spent some time watching how the other marques were doing, particularly the new Lotus and the new McLaren, which was remarkable for its carbon-fibre shell.

After the Long Beach episode, I spun out again in Spain, after a driving error that was entirely of my own making.

But the season is worth recalling for the good moments – and, believe me, there were plenty of those. In Argentina, I made it to the winner's podium for the first time, behind Nelson Piquet – who was destined to win his first world championship at the end of the year – and Carlos Reutemann.

Then I won my first Grand Prix.

Winning your first Grand Prix is a passport to the future. Which is a way of saying that, once you have won a Grand Prix, you are free from all the inhibitions and complexes that have held you back. You know that you are every bit as good as those around you, and Formula One takes on an entirely new aspect. You have climbed a mountain which, only the night before, appeared insurmountable.

49

You are a winner, you go into the record books, and you have the impression – totally warranted by the way – that the world now sees you in a different light.

It happened in Dijon. It was the French Grand Prix, a race that was probably more important to Renault than any other on the calendar.

Fifth of July. The sky in Burgundy is black. After forty-eight laps, the race is interrupted by a cloudburst. Restart. Only twenty-two laps to go. Soft slicks on the Renault now, unlike Piquet, who has changed tyres but kept to the same compound. Will the slicks last the distance? Maybe not, but they will certainly be faster in the early laps, especially since the circuit is still quite wet. It is a risk, but it is a calculated risk. It comes off. I beat Piquet to the line.

The Brabhams of that year – Nelson's included – tended to bend the regulations. Gordon Murray had fitted them with a hydro-pneumatic suspension which dropped the car the moment it was in motion and, essentially, restored ground effect. This was clearly against the rules but, since it was impossible to measure ground clearance in a moving Formula One machine, Brabham got away with it.

The most fiery, the most powerful – I would even go as far as to say, the most violent – driver that year was unquestionably Alan Jones. One quality I particularly admired in him was his handling of the Williams in the first few laps of a race, when his tanks were still full. It was no coincidence that he was the reigning world champion.

We had already squared off against each other on numerous occasions. Two months after the French Grand Prix, we were running neck-and-neck in the Dutch Grand Prix at Zandvoort. I had secured pole position and I was in the lead, but Alan kept coming back at me. We had been locked together like this once before, in the German Grand Prix, and that time he had got the upper hand.

After ten laps of Zandvoort, he was breathing my exhaust fumes, and he finally squeezed past on lap eighteen. When you have been battling it out like that, the driver who comes through from behind often inflicts a telling blow to your morale. Jones was doubtlessly counting on this being the case, and his concentration wavered. Five hundred metres on, as we were braking down for the Tarzan Corner, I pulled alongside him and forced my way back into the lead. This took him completely by surprise and he made no effort

Seen here with (from left to right) Gérard Larrousse, Bernard Hanon, then CEO at Renault, and René Arnoux on a memorable day in Dijon at the French Grand Prix. I have just won my first Formula One event

On the podium, this time with Piquet and Watson

to shut me out. I was in front again and I held my lead to win my second Grand Prix.

That win was even more important than the one in Dijon. The battle of wills with Jones, the reigning world champion, hadn't done my reputation any harm in the eyes of the spectators.

My third Grand Prix win, this time at Monza, came hot on the heels of my victory at Zandvoort. My team-mate René Arnoux started in pole position, but I took over at the first chicane and led all the way to the finishing line.

At the end of that season, I was the happiest of men. I was in my second year of Formula One, I was in a top team for the first time, and I had come through with flying colours – fifth place in the world championship behind Piquet, Reutemann, Jones and Laffite. I had achieved two pole positions, three Grands Prix wins, twice runner-up, and one third place – in all, six trips to the podium. I had attracted attention in my passage of arms with Jones, I had led the Canadian Grand Prix in pouring rain (proof that the Renault Turbo wasn't the only factor contributing to my success) and, to cap it all, I had outperformed my team-mate René Arnoux in much the same way as I had bested John Watson the season before.

Granted, René had driven to four pole positions, but he hadn't won a Grand Prix all season, and I am certain that I could have matched his performance in qualifying if Gérard Larrousse had given me the green light – which he didn't always do. I remember being absolutely livid in England when I came in after driving the fastest qualifying lap and Larrousse immediately sent René out again with the turbo boost turned up higher.

I was quite prepared to sign up with Renault for the 1982 championship season, but there were strings attached and I was determined to pull them.

Life in Saint Chamond had also changed in the interim. Nicolas was born on 18 August, 1981, on the eve of the Dutch Grand Prix: a new and enormously important person in my life.

9 *Twelve months too long*

Anne-Marie, Nicolas and a Formula One career that was beginning to take shape: taken together, these elements meant I was in top physical and mental condition to tackle the 1982 season.

What I hadn't realised was that, up until now, life had handled me with kid gloves.

1982 was a shitty year. There is no other word for it: it was a sluggish, irritating and, worse still, tragic year.

For all that, it started off with a flourish. I was leading the first Grand Prix of the season – in South Africa – when my rear left tyre blew. I made it back to the pits, changing gears as little as possible because there were only a few strips of rubber left on the rim. I changed all four tyres, launched myself out of the pits, and drove aggressively enough to take the lead a few laps from home. I finished first.

This was unheard of in Formula One. Up to then, no-one had made a pit stop and gone on to win a Grand Prix. In fact, I had just demonstrated that, with a good pit crew (the guys at Renault were exceptionally talented) and with a good car, you could come in to the pits during the race and still go back out and win.

The implications of this incident were not lost on Bernie Ecclestone or Gordon Murray over at Brabham. After what must have been considerable soul-searching, they announced one day to the absolute stupefaction of the other teams that, in future, the Brabhams would be waved into the pits in the middle of the race to refuel and change tyres. The advantage? Quite simply, that they would be more competitive racing a lighter car with fresher tyres.

The gambit paid dividends until refuelling was outlawed because of the threat to safety it implied. To this day, tyre changes are still a feature. I would add that this is the only positive contribution made by the 1982 season, because those pit stops made Formula One decidedly more exciting.

South Africa – and a Formula One 'first': I blow a tyre, drive back to the pits, change tyres, and come back out to win. This is what inspired the Brabham team to inaugurate refuelling in mid-race . . .

That apart, the rest of 1982 was a nightmare. For one thing, there was all that rubbish about a super-licence. Now that they had ironed out their differences, FISA and FOCA got together in Kyalami in South Africa and came up with the notion that the drivers should sign a document which was intended purely and simply to tie their hands and give the individual team bosses control over transfer rights.

The drivers went on strike to protest against the proposed system. Didier Pironi and his lawyers acted as our spokesmen, and Niki Lauda – who had just come out of retirement to join McLaren – contributed invaluable moral support.

The Kyalami drivers' strike was an unforgettable experience. We barricaded ourselves into our hotel, all together in the same room (to make sure that there were no defectors). De Angelis played the piano, Villeneuve made the rounds of the younger drivers to keep their morale high, and Giacomelli coached us on the finer points of Italian terrorist tactics.

54

The FISA/FOCA super-licence scheme proved to be a non-starter.

The next thing about 1982 was the blatant cheating that went on. As the turbos became progressively more competitive, some teams went to astonishing lengths to circumvent weight restrictions. The water-container ploy was probably the most distasteful. In theory, the cars carried water to help cool the brakes. In fact, the water pods were emptied soon after the start of the race, the result being that the teams which had them were running some thirty to forty kilos lighter than their competitors. Once they crossed the finishing line, the pods were refilled with water (the current regulations provided for fluids to be topped-up) and, lo and behold, the cars were back at their qualifying weight.

The ploy sometimes backfired. There were disqualifications, subsequently upheld by the FIA Tribunal, including those of Piquet and Rosberg in Brazil. As I happened to be lying third at the finish, I suddenly found myself back in the record books as the winner of the 1982 Brazilian Grand Prix.

After that decision, the FOCA teams boycotted the San Marino Grand Prix, which left the field open to the top independent teams

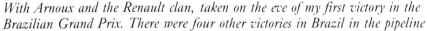

With Arnoux and the Renault clan, taken on the eve of my first victory in the Brazilian Grand Prix. There were four other victories in Brazil in the pipeline

Keke Rosberg, 1982 Formula One World Champion

Renault and Ferrari. The drivers' strike had been followed by a constructors' strike.

To win that particular world championship, you had to have a heart of steel and a car to match it. That season, there were no fewer than eleven winners in sixteen Grands Prix. I won two of them myself (the South African and the Brazilian), as did Pironi, Watson, Lauda and Arnoux, whereas De Angelis, Rosberg, Tambay, Alboreto, Patrese and Piquet scored one win apiece. Rosberg took the championship because he had the most reliable car, a quality that was conspicuously absent in the Renault – I failed to finish on eight separate occasions.

The Renault team had problems of its own, the most public of these being a clash between René Arnoux and myself which occurred at the French Grand Prix at Paul Ricard. I have repeatedly been taken to task over this episode, because I was identified as the villain of the piece. The fact that I have not always been a favourite in France is largely due to this affair – or, rather, to my honest account of what happened.

René and I were together on the first row of the grid. Gérard Larrousse told René to let me through if the two of us were among the points coming up to finish, the rationale being that I was ahead of René in the world championship. I must stress that I didn't make any such request to René or to Gérard Larrousse, simply because if I had been in René's shoes, I would have refused point-blank.

René didn't protest against Larrousse's instructions. Once the race got under way, he moved into the lead and I tagged along behind him, not forcing the pace, just nursing the car along. I was following instructions to the letter. What I didn't know was that, deep down, René had not found it in himself to do the same. If only he had said something, a quick word of warning, I would have made sure that he didn't build up a lead of some twenty seconds. When the pits flashed a signal to him – '1. Prost 2. Arnoux' – he didn't ease up. And I didn't have enough time left to come back at him.

In the light of subsequent experience, I have to say that Gérard Larrousse was crazy even to propose such an arrangement, let alone imagine that it might work. Not least, because it totally misconstrued the way a racing driver's mind functions. Still, the

Arnoux and I didn't see eye to eye in the 1982 French Grand Prix. Pironi was third

damage had been done and, in the heat of the moment, I felt cheated. And I certainly gave vent to my anger once we had crossed the line. For me, Arnoux had welshed on the deal and the race had been a sham. And it seemed worthwhile making that clear. But telling the truth isn't always the smartest thing to do.

The icing on the cake was when I was on my way home from Paul Ricard. I pulled into a gas station to fill up for the ride back to Saint Chamond and, for some reason or other, the attendant mistook me for Arnoux. 'Well done, M. Arnoux! That Prost is a proper little prick – he had it coming.' I was livid. I whipped out some cash – I could hardly use a credit card, since my name would be on it – paid him and burnt rubber out of there. So much for the view of Joe Public.

Needless to say, René and I buried that particular hatchet a long time ago. Today, our relationship is one of comradeship and mutual respect. In any case, the incident – which was blown up out of all proportion – was no more than a footnote to the 1982 championship season. There was much, much worse to come.

It was raining heavily at Hockenheim during practice for the German Grand Prix. I was taking it very easy. Didier Pironi's Ferrari came up behind me at speed. By that stage of the season, he was a serious championship contender and he was clearly determined to get as much practice as he could in the wet in case of rain on the Sunday of the race. Pironi ploughed into the back of me. His Ferrari shot up in the air and smashed down again on the track. Didier was seriously injured. He almost lost the use of his legs and it was many weeks before he could walk again. That shunt marked the end of his driving career. In 1987, as he was planning his comeback in Formula One, he was killed in a powerboat race.

Ricardo Paletti had already been killed in the previous race, the Canadian Grand Prix. Pironi had trouble getting away and Paletti came steaming through from the back of the grid and crashed straight into him at speed. He was a victim of his own inexperience: it was his second start in Formula One.

Then, on 8 May, 1982, our friend Gilles Villeneuve was killed during practice for the Belgian Grand Prix at Zolder. His career had been brief, but he had left his mark on the sport. He will always be remembered for his exceptional driving skills, his sincerity and his unbounded generosity. He was a very fine person, a living legend, and everyone in Formula One liked and respected him. As Enzo Ferrari used to say: 'Villeneuve the Great.' 1982 had been a shitty year.

10 *Pipped by Piquet*

The Renault team went through another reshuffle at the end of 1982. The company had been involved in Formula One since 1977 and management wanted results – not just a win here and there, but a world championship title. Everyone at Renault Sport HQ in Viry-Chatillon was fired up. And so was I.

My status within the team had changed. I was the number one driver and Eddie Cheever had been brought in as number two. I now had a much more important role to play than previously. In addition to driving, I had acquired responsibility for testing and setting up the cars. I had also become a standard-bearer for Renault, in the sense that I was involved in all manner of PR and promotional campaigns.

This was an entirely new departure for me and, with the benefit of hindsight, I have to say that my lack of experience in this area meant that I didn't fully appreciate the issues and techniques involved. It seemed to me that I was permanently on call on one pretext or another, when what I needed most was to channel my physical and mental efforts into my *real* profession. I am convinced that, with a few more years' experience in Formula One, I would have reacted very differently to the extra-curricular demands made on me by Renault, which ranged all the way from low-key factory visits to high-profile personal appearances, not to mention press conferences and receptions at most Grand Prix venues.

What is more, as the season wore on, there seemed to be a lot of in-fighting at Renault. And, instead of letting the professionals get on with it, some of Renault's senior management began to interfere in certain key decisions relating to the team. Some of the briefings were stormy and everyone, myself included, was beginning to get edgy.

I was only really happy behind the wheel. I didn't make too many mistakes in 1983. In fact, I don't believe I had ever driven as well before that year. I was sharp, I was stretching the limits of the car, and, at the same time, I was cutting risks to a minimum. I won four of the season's fifteen Grands Prix, I was placed second twice and third once. I failed to finish in three races, one of them being the Dutch Grand Prix at Zandvoort.

If I single out Zandvoort, it is because of the protracted debate that followed an error of judgment involving Nelson Piquet, who was at that stage my direct rival for the title. I spun out after clipping Nelson and sending him off into the shrubbery.

It was by no means the first mistake I had made in Formula One, but there had always been a reason. Except perhaps in Monaco in 1982, where I smashed into the rails a few laps from the finish when I was out in front and in the clear. There had been some drops of rain and the track conditions were constantly changing, but it was never quite established whether the fault was mine. In fact, coming

The Renault RE-40 was a superb car

out of the chicane, I felt something go at the back and it could have been a broken differential.

The circumstances at Zandvoort were completely different. I was seen as the culprit, above all because I had come up too fast on Piquet. From my vantage point in the cockpit, it was a completely different ball-game. First of all, Nelson's Brabham had the edge over my Renault on the straight. I was able to come back at him in the corners, but I knew that it would be unbelievably difficult to pass him. I had to catch him off guard. And it was imperative that I beat him because I knew that, as the season progressed, the Brabham would be improving all the time and that he would have a definite advantage over me in the closing races of the championship.

There was another point everybody ignored. Arnoux's Ferrari was coming up fast behind us because, overall, the Brabham was holding me up. And René was also a serious title contender.

In the final analysis, the shunt at Zandvoort wasn't as crucial as everyone made out, because it left Piquet and myself level pegging. I'd had to push things along a bit and I'd blown it. That was that.

The Italian Grand Prix came next. And, once again, tempers became frayed – although this time for a different reason.

My position at Renault, the firm's diligent PR efforts on my behalf, and the fact that I was winning races had combined to make me the focus of French motor racing. I had become – albeit unwillingly – a star. Being a star has certain media advantages, but it also has all sorts of drawbacks. At home in Saint Chamond, I was being inundated with all kinds of requests, not to mention anonymous telephone calls and even threats. The situation was making life increasingly difficult for Anne-Marie and Nicolas. I hit on the idea of moving abroad. Accordingly, I made the necessary overtures to the Swiss authorities in 1983 and, in May of that year, I moved house, cutting my ties with France.

Before the Italian Grand Prix I received more anonymous letters and, worse still, kidnapping threats. Renault took the precaution of hiring three French police officers, security specialists assigned to the French President, to look after me. Unfortunately, the story leaked and – not surprisingly – the Italian press and the Monza public took umbrage. I was even more unpopular than before.

Piquet won the next-to-last race of the season, the European Grand Prix at Brands Hatch, and I was runner-up for the second time that year. I was still two points ahead of Piquet in the title race – 57 to 55.

SOUTHERN SUN HOTELS
SOUTHERN SUN HOTELS
SOUTHERN SUN HOTELS
FILA
parmalat
Parmalat
FILA
HARIBO
Marlboro

There was just one more race to come in the 1983 world championship, the South African Grand Prix. The title was still wide open.

There was no point in getting my hopes up – that would have been a futile exercise in self-deception. I spent a few days away from it all on Nelson's boat. I faced up to the facts. Only good luck – or, more likely, bad luck on Nelson's part – could see me through.

I had been sounding the alarm *chez* Renault ever since my fourth and last win of the season in the Austrian Grand Prix. No-one was better-placed than myself to vouch for the remarkable progress made by the Brabham and, above all, its BMW turbo engine. I wasn't at all convinced that the Renault people had a grasp on the problem (other than the drivers, who knew the score), but it was real and there for all to see. Our turbos came from the same supplier as BMW, and there was a question-mark over the fuel Brabham was using and whether it was within the rules.

I was very depressed. I could see my title hopes evaporating and I knew that an opportunity to win a world championship doesn't come along too often.

As things turned out, the South African Grand Prix was absolute torture. On the thirty-sixth lap, with Piquet blithely hammering along, I heard a distinctive snort-cum-splutter from my engine, an unmistakable sign that a turbo had packed in. I drove into the pits, got out, and watched from the side of the track. There was still a possibility that Piquet might not finish. But he eased home comfortably in third place and claimed his second world championship.

Piquet 59, Prost 57.

There was some talk – via François Guiter at Elf, for instance – of lodging a protest against Brabham on account of the fuel they had used. The Renault management was opposed to this, first of all for reasons of corporate image and, secondly, because certain people didn't see any point in standing up for me. I later found out why: Renault and I were on the point of parting company.

Some nights are tough to get through. The night of 15 October in South Africa was one.

Opposite: *Image of defeat, South Africa, 1983. The Renault team didn't measure up. Nelson Piquet* (left) *wins the title in a Brabham-BMW designed by Gordon Murray* (centre)

11 *Farewell to Renault*

Formula One teams have their seasonal ups and downs. That is a fact of life in motor racing. Some never really make it and disappear from the scene for good, only for others to appear in their stead.

The one exception appears to be Ferrari, which has somehow always managed to keep its head above water. Lotus and Tyrrell have both known what life is like in the doldrums after spending several seasons on the crest of the wave. And the same holds true for McLaren: after two world championship titles with Emerson Fittipaldi in 1974 and James Hunt in 1976, the team founded by Bruce McLaren went into a pronounced downward spiral and hit rock bottom when first Patrick Tambay and then myself and other novices were on board.

When I left McLaren for Renault at the end of 1980, the fortunes of the McLaren team were at a turning point, thanks to the calculated intervention of Philip Morris Europe, i.e. Marlboro, which had made up its mind to take things in hand. The European subsidiary of Philip Morris is behind the sponsorship which underwrites Marlboro's financial commitment to Formula One. John Hogan, who is the man in charge of finance, simply couldn't stand by and watch substantial past commitments go down the drain.

John was on extremely good terms with a reliable man who had amply demonstrated that he knew what he was doing: Ron Dennis. Ron had started out as a pit mechanic and had worked his way up to the position of team manager thanks to his technical and racing experience on the one hand, and his managerial flair on the other. Together with another technician, Neil Trundle, he had set up Rondel Racing – and had even flirted with Formula One with the Motul M1. After that, he had put together the Project Team, which developed into Project Three and Project Four.

Above left: Brands
Hatch, 1985: a
champagne
tribute to a first
world title

Above right:
Showering the fans,
not to mention
each other, is a
drivers' tradition
I am happy to
continue!

Right: The French
connection – Laffite
improvises
transportation in
Canada. Tambay
and Alliot are along
for the ride

Above: The McLaren team in 1986.
Keke Rosberg was a staunch team-mate

Left: I dislike Detroit, despite the décor

Below: Hungary, 1986 – no happy
memories of this race; not a good
course to drive

Above: Practice in the rain

Overleaf: The German Grand Prix,
1986. I ran out of fuel a few metres
from the finishing line. I was livid

Above: Australia, 1986: it has just dawned on me that I am world champion for the second time

Previous page: Adelaide, 1986: that chequered flag signals victory in the Australian Grand Prix – and a second world championship title

John Hogan knew that Ron would make a success of running a racing Formula One squad, and that he would stay within budget. Accordingly, at the end of 1980, a time when Marlboro had acquired a major say in matters at McLaren – John put Ron Dennis in to manage the team. A little later, Teddy Mayer was moved on.

When Ron came to McLaren, he discovered a kindred spirit in John Barnard. More important, both of them were sufficiently ambitious and level-headed to clear out the dead wood and start with a clean slate. John had already done some work on a very interesting project: a Formula One superstructure in carbon fibre and other composite materials. This shell promised to have distinct advantages over traditional aluminium alloy superstructures.

The new McLaren made its debut in 1981. It was significant that it did not continue the M23, M24, M29, M30 series: its official designation was the MP4, symbolising the partnership between Marlboro and McLaren at Project Four. The MP4 won only once that season, when John Watson carried off the British Grand Prix, but that success meant that McLaren was back in business.

I suggested earlier that Ron Dennis and John Barnard had ambitions, that they didn't cling to outmoded values and that they weren't afraid to innovate. In two vital instances, they proved in flamboyant fashion that this was true.

In 1982, they released De Cesaris and chose a new team-mate for John Watson. Not just any old world champion, not one of the up-and-coming youngsters. No way. They chose Lauda. Niki still had the bug. But he had to find out for himself if he still had what it takes to make a comeback. He tried out under conditions of utmost secrecy. Ron Dennis had got himself the most celebrated racing driver of the day.

Ron and John went about things in much the same way when it came to choosing an engine for the new McLaren. The turbo era was more or less at its peak and the normally-aspirated engine had just about breathed its last, as both BMW and Renault had so convincingly demonstrated.

Once again, Ron Dennis took the bull by the horns. He linked up with Mansour Ojjeh and his firm Techniques d'Avant-Garde (TAG). And there was no question of Ojjeh working with any old do-it-yourself outfit: he, in turn, had to have the best that was available. He chose Porsche. The new McLaren-TAG-Porsche made its first appearance at the end of the 1983 championship season, at the Dutch Grand Prix, in a dress rehearsal for 1984.

65

John Barnard had insisted on three parameters being respected by Hans Mezger, Porsche's project director at Weissach: the width, length and height of the future V6 turbo. After that, Mezger was on his own.

What I didn't suspect at the time was that I would share in McLaren's extraordinary success.

While all this was happening at McLaren, I was beginning to get angry with Renault. Renault Sport had been favourite for the 1983 championship, and our defeat had been hard to swallow. Moreover, as was often the case with Renault, it was the drivers who had to shoulder much of the responsibility for failure.

The situation was degenerating into personal squabbles. Eddie Cheever apparently wasn't performing up to scratch, so his fate was sealed even before the South African Grand Prix. As for myself, the position was deteriorating day by day.

For Renault, the sole priority – and I could appreciate this – was the well-being of the company. But I kept trying to get through to the Renault Sport management down in Viry-Chatillon that Formula One was first and foremost a *drivers'* championship, a flesh-and-blood issue, if you like, and not just a question of cars. As a result, I argued, Renault would stand to benefit immeasurably if yours truly became world champion driving one of their cars.

There was no convincing them. I simply couldn't get the message across. It seemed there were certain categorical imperatives emanating from Renault HQ in Boulogne-Billancourt that could not be ignored.

I remember one episode in the 1982 season that amply illustrates the dimensions of the problem. We knew from way back that the performance and reliability of a turbo-charged engine hinged on the electronic system which controlled fuel feed and ignition. There were systems on the market which had demonstrated their viability. But Renault had a subsidiary called Renix which was involved in research and development of a similar system, and there was no way that Bernard Dudot, our technical engineer, could turn to an outside manufacturer. As things stood, we would have to wait until Renix had achieved a breakthrough. I know that the Renix R and D people were working their tails off, but while they were doing so, other teams were winning Formula One races.

To cut a long story short, it was patently obvious on the day after the South African Grand Prix, when we had just missed out on the championship title, that Renault and I were about to part company.

To anyone who had one ounce of perception, it was a foregone conclusion, as was proved only days later.

Once I had 'resigned' from Renault, I asked everyone concerned to keep my departure under wraps for a few days to give me a chance to develop my contacts with other teams with a view to the 1984 championship season. The very next day after Kyalami, I was shattered to read an article in *L'Equipe* which predicted that Renault and Prost were splitting up.

My first thought was that Johnny Rives, who had written the article, had been told – more or less on the record – about the goings-on behind the scenes. That wasn't the case. In the plane back from Johannesburg, my friends Johnny and Jean-Louis had been chatting with Jean-Pierre Hanrioud (who, at that time, was in charge of the Renault caravan division) and they had analysed the pertinent facts of the situation, with which they were fully familiar. Without any other concrete information at their disposal, they had come to the inescapable conclusion: the situation was beyond repair. The only issue which remained to be resolved between Renault and myself would be not if, but *when*.

Meanwhile, the first person to suffer because of that insightful article in *L'Equipe* was Alain Prost. There was no hope now of negotiating with Ron Dennis on the same basis as our informal discussion a few weeks previously. Ron is a shrewd businessman. He knew that it was no longer a question of tempting me away from Renault. It was only a matter of taking me on at McLaren. And McLaren didn't have a Formula One vacancy at that point.

I had my feathers well and truly ruffled in the negotiations that ensued. Strangely enough, although I have a reputation for being grasping, I didn't really care. Quite the opposite. I was pleased to have extricated myself from a hostile situation. I was tired.

I wanted *out*.

12 *Teaming up with a legend*

By some miracle, life seemed much simpler as soon as I donned the red and white racing colours of Marlboro McLaren.

Before test-driving the car, I had to go to the workshops at Woking in England to have my seat made and get acquainted with a new cockpit. At Woking, I came across Niki Lauda who – in his own fashion – gave me a genuinely warm welcome. In one of his books, Niki mentions that, when we first came together at McLaren, he kept a watchful eye on me because I seemed to be keeping a watchful eye on him. In my case, that was understandable. After all, this was *the* Niki Lauda, in my view one of the finest drivers of all time. And it would have been silly of me not to keep an eye on him, assessing his reactions and his analytical approach to problem-solving.

After my first trip to Woking, there were a couple of PR obligations to fulfil and that was all. I spent a long vacation with Anne-Marie back in Switzerland, most of the time spent looking for the house that was destined to become the Prost family home.

We finally decided on a place in Yens, in one of the most beautiful parts of Switzerland – a rambling, ramshackle affair that we could gradually convert to our taste. I bought it at the end of 1984 and we have lived there since October 1985.

One fine day in November 1983, Ron Dennis rang to tell me to come down to Paul Ricard for initial trials in the McLaren MP4/2. This was the version of the McLaren-TAG-Porsche which

The McLaren team, 1984

followed the one Lauda had first driven the previous season in the Dutch Grand Prix.

I drove down to Paul Ricard in my Mercedes 500 SEC coupé. After all, there was no clause in my present contract which obliged me to drive a Renault.

I was back behind the wheel. I was happy. I had turned over yet another new leaf.

13 *Meet the crew*

Niki Lauda was already in Le Castellet when I arrived. Niki had been the first driver to try out the original McLaren-TAG-Porsche, so it was only natural that he take the latest model for a spin to gauge how well the transition had been made from prototype to definitive version.

Then it was my turn to drive the McLaren.

If the car's lap times and handling were anything to go by, it seemed sound, but we would have to wait until it had been put through its paces under Formula One race conditions before we could really judge how good the McLaren was. Having said that, the engine was positively astonishing. Its power and pick-up were very impressive indeed and – as we were to confirm throughout the championship season that followed – it was remarkably adaptable to every kind of circuit, fast or slow, at altitude or at sea-level.

Porsche's technicians and the people from Bosch had worked in close harmony to develop their joint 'Motronic' programme, as they had chosen to call the onboard mini-computer system used to correlate instantly the vast amount of pertinent data and to co-ordinate ignition, fuel feed and injection functions. The fundamental advantages of such a system cannot be stressed too emphatically.

The international governing body had accepted that something had to be done to curb the seemingly limitless power being developed by supercharged engines. Its response was draconian: in future, Formula One fuel capacity would be restricted to 220 litres. A similar rule already applied to endurance racing with sports-car prototypes where, incidentally, Porsche and Bosch had also worked in close co-operation and now dominated the market. That augured well for the future.

While I was coming to terms with the McLaren, I also had an opportunity to get to know the members of the team.

John Barnard was a proficient engineer – an unassuming fellow with an easy smile, who was nonetheless punctilious, not to say manic, in technical matters. He was both creative and imaginative. And there was just the slightest hint of the xenophobe: for him, there tended to be the English, then everybody else. However, since I am also rather conservative, I may well have made a reasonable impression on him. Be that as it may, there were good vibes between us although, as the years passed, I found him unduly obstinate on occasion (which can be both good and bad).

Barnard had assembled around himself strong technical back-up from the likes of Alan Jenkins, Tim Wright and Steve Nichols, all of them people I was destined to work with closely in the years ahead.

The man who ran the show did so with authority, perspicacity and composure. For Ron Dennis, the team had to be absolutely immaculate right down the line, not only as regards performance and results, but also in terms of how the cars and pit crew were turned out. Like any experienced businessman, he also knew how to draw up a comprehensive budget *and* respect it to the letter. I have often heard Ron Dennis say that his is less of a 'hands-on' managerial approach than that of his counterparts in other top teams, and my own experience of him suggests that this is true. He would get together with John Barnard, define an action programme and unequivocally follow it through. By comparison with Renault, for example, our test programme that season was negligible, not counting the occasional tyre trials conducted by FOCA immediately before a number of Grands Prix.

Being involved in that tyre-testing programme even before the beginning of the season proper allowed me to confirm under quasi-competitive conditions that the McLaren was a very sound machine – and a very comfortable drive. I drove series after series of incredibly fast lap times with no great effort at all.

While these trials were going on, I was beginning to settle into the team. Lauda and I were on an equal footing – each of us had his own clearly-defined priorities and programme. Niki worked with Tim Wright as his technician, and I had Alan Jenkins. Niki and I took it in turn to drive the reserve car and our team effort was well-balanced.

Along the way, I was introduced to Niki's personal physiotherapist, Willy Dungl, who was also to spend an increasing amount of time on me as the season wore on. Although Willy himself doesn't

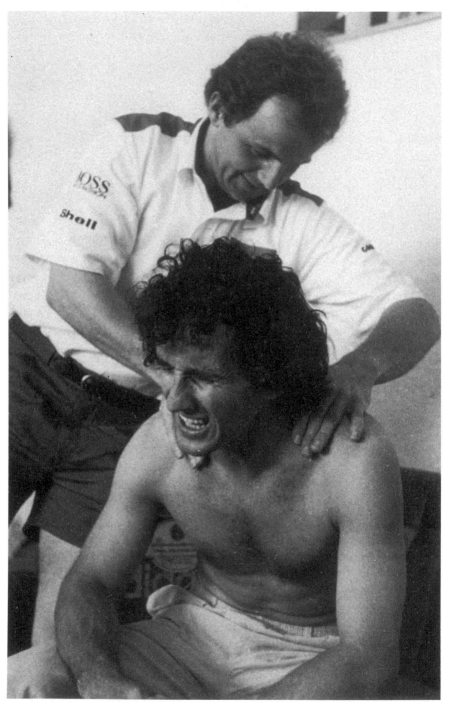

Joseph, my physiotherapist: hands of steel

Jacques Laffite – a friend for all seasons

frequent the circuits any more, I am still in the hands of one or other of his 'disciples'. Willy's daughter Andrea took up where he left off and, when she married, Joseph stepped into her shoes, as of the 1988 season. With Joseph, there is absolutely no chance of transgressing against the dietary regime decreed by Willy: fish, milk products and a strict ban on spirits.

My private life was also taking on new dimensions. I now seemed to have much more free time to spend with friends, particularly with Jacques Laffite. In the previous few months, Jacques and I had come to realise that we had a lot of interests in common – above all, golf, not to mention our shared passion for cards. We instituted marathon games of *belote 'Gordini'* – a variant of pinochle devised (according to Johnny Rives) by Amédée Gordini – which developed into an interminable Formula One world *belote* championship, successive rounds of which are played at every Grand Prix.

Our crowd also developed a taste for horsing around, stopping (just) short or rowdyism. We were always in each other's company at races, until Jacques had his shunt at Brands in 1986, which ended his Formula One career. As a result, we obviously see rather less of each other in a racing context – Jacques is in the touring class and I am still in Formula One – added to which is the fact that Jacques doesn't like coming to Grand Prix events because they bring back too many fond memories and rekindle his urge to get back into a single-seater. For all that, we continue to see a lot of each other when we are on vacation or whenever I stop over in Paris.

14 *A successful Formula*

1984 was a dramatic, electrifying, unpredictable, nail-biting year: a magnificent championship season which, to my mind at least, showed Formula One at its best.

I won the first race of the season, the Brazilian Grand Prix. I set off cautiously, trying to get the measure of the car on that particular circuit – trying it on for size, you might say. Alboreto's Ferrari, Lauda in the other McLaren and Warwick's Renault held the top three positions for lap after lap, and I didn't squeeze past them until we were on the fifty-first lap. I had to keep one eye permanently on my fuel gauge – this would soon become second-nature to us all, but Brazil was the first time we had ever raced under the new fuel restrictions. However, I eased home quite comfortably.

I remember that Grand Prix as if it were only a few hours ago. As Gordon Murray (McLaren's technical director since 1987) will confirm, memory is one of my strong points. I remember virtually every detail of every race I have ever driven, including qualifying laps against the clock. If someone says 'Brazil '84,' I can reel off lap times, tyre compounds and set-up positions – how I angled the rear wing or the front flap and how the car responded.

The minute I got out of the car in Brazil, they swarmed round me: 'That's one in the eye for Renault', that sort of thing. I was too elated to comment. I had delivered the goods in my first outing with a new team and I now looked forward to a straightforward season without any real problems.

The relationship between Lauda and myself became closer, particularly after the second Grand Prix of the season in Kyalami. As I said, it had been decided up front that Niki and I would each do our own thing, taking it in turn to look after the reserve car, and then compare notes during pre-race briefing sessions.

Time was short in South Africa, however, so we had to work in

On tour. My mother and father (centre) *on a visit to Canada*

tandem. Niki took charge of the engines and I assumed responsibility for setting up. That way, we could get all the cars ready in time. We complemented each other perfectly: for one whole day, we unreservedly exchanged every item of information we uncovered.

Niki is a delightful person, once you get to know him, with a great sense of humour and a real lust for life. And it was a joy to work alongside someone whose arguments were so precise and lucid. Better still, our driving styles and our approach to technical problems were similar. You couldn't wish for a better partner.

Niki won in South Africa. I went off too fast in the reserve car (which, by the way, Niki had prepared extremely well).

Prost and McLaren in Brazil, Lauda and McLaren in South Africa: the opening races had promptly confirmed what we had suspected before the season began. The McLaren was in great shape.

1984 was a triumphant year for the McLaren-TAG-Porsche stable. Of the sixteen Grands Prix, there were only two where both Niki and myself failed to finish – at Zolder and in Dallas. The rest of the year was a succession of wins or, at worse, world championship point finishes.

At Zolder, our technicians couldn't find the right permutation of fuel grade and injection programme; as the turbos became increasingly powerful, the question of fuel grade was becoming progressively more important.

As for Dallas, in what was at best a parody of a Grand Prix, the circuit simply disintegrated and both Niki and I were among those who finished up in the concrete walls lining the circuit. It has to be said that scheduling that Grand Prix in Dallas took some nerve, both on the part of the US race organisers, who obviously thought all they had to do was stake out a course between two concrete walls erected in a cornfield, and on the part of Bernie Ecclestone, who gave them the green light. Attempting to put on a Grand Prix under those conditions was absolutely scandalous. And the hit-or-miss organisation was also a disgrace. The drivers were inches away from calling a strike, and Laffite was all set to make his feelings plain in his own inimitable way by turning up for qualifying between seven and eight on Sunday morning, still dressed in his pyjamas.

1984 also stands out in my memory because of three close calls in very tight situations.

First of all was the San Marino Grand Prix at Imola. I had led from the start and was about thirty seconds up on Derek Warwick. Carbon brake discs are lighter and, in the medium-term at least, more effective than their traditional counterparts, but we weren't nearly as familiar with them then as we are today. One unfortunate characteristic that we hadn't been able to handle up to that point was their unpredictable performance when they heated up. What is more, brake pedal travel varied constantly. At any rate, I was just coming up to one of the most tricky braking manoeuvres of the season, approaching the Tosa Corner. To appreciate how difficult it is, you only have to think back to some highly memorable exits at Tosa – Villeneuve, Scheckter, or (more recently) Piquet in 1987, when he left the imprint of his Williams on the safety rail. I came into Tosa and hit the brakes. All the way down to the boards. Zero. The only thing I produced was a flamboyant spin at top speed. By some miracle, the car came out of the spin pointing in exactly the right direction. After that, the brakes came back on again, so to speak, and I crossed the finishing line in first place a few laps later.

A second close call came at the French Grand Prix in Dijon. It was a brake problem once again, but not the same as at Imola. And it nearly turned out very nasty. I was lying second behind Tambay as we came downhill at speed into the banked Pouas Curve, when suddenly, just as we were levelling out and the car was drifting wide, the offside wheel front left began to shudder, then to detach itself. I managed to slow down and get the McLaren under control again, but it was weaving from side to side. I had barely enough momentum to reach the safety of the pit lane. A really nasty situation.

The third serious incident that season meant a hasty exit for me from a particularly fast circuit, the Österreichring. After some twenty laps, the overworked fourth-gear pinion began to show signs of wear-and-tear. The gears had already slipped out on several occasions and I had been forced to hold fourth in with my right hand. In spite of that, I had managed to close on Piquet and was right on his tail. I was matching him gear for gear as we were swallowed up in the Rindt Curve, the long and impressive righthander which comes before the grandstand straight. Shortly before, De Angelis had blown his engine and left a large oil slick on the tarmac. Piquet saw it and swerved in the nick of time. But I was riveted to his tailpipe and couldn't see a thing. When I did see the oil, it was too late. A split second later I was bang up against the rail, unscathed, but out of the running.

While all this was going on, Niki was riding high, with skill – and a little bit of luck – on his side. In Austria, just like me, he heard a sinister clunk from his gearbox. He was on the brink of retiring, but he was a long way from the pits, so he fiddled around among the gears to see if there was one left to coast home on. And he found one, then a second, then a third. And kept going. And won.

Thanks to that clever win in Austria, Niki moved into first position in the world championship, with 48 points, 2·5 points ahead of me.

This half-point is perhaps a little puzzling until you remember that sudden torrential rain had brought the Monaco Grand Prix to a premature end. I had been in the lead when the race was declared over. Jacky Ickx – himself a masterful driver in the wet – was the course director, and he didn't have a moment's hesitation in bringing down the chequered flag on the thirty-first of seventy-seven laps. The regulations provided that the drivers in race order from one to six would receive half the points awarded for a full Grand Prix. I had won, but I only picked up four-and-a-half points. There is no need to dwell on the hullabaloo that ensued. Suffice it to say that Senna had been directly behind me in the Toleman, very well-placed to challenge for his first Grand Prix victory, so there was reportedly a near-riot in Brazil. Then there were serious differences of opinion between the Automobile Club of Monaco and FISA, which couldn't bring itself to pass up such a golden oportunity to make a mountain out of a molehill. Jacky Ickx took a lot of stick although his decision had been beyond reproach.

When the dust settled, Lauda was leading the championship and there were only four more races left. I did my utmost to catch him, winning both the Dutch Grand Prix and the European Grand Prix, held that year at Nürburgring. Unfortunately, mechanical failure put me out of the next race, the Italian Grand Prix at Monza.

I was still in with a chance. Niki was on 66 points and I was on 62·5, with one race to go – the Portuguese Grand Prix. My options were limited: I had to win. And, if I did, Niki would have to come second to take the title.

I like the Estoril circuit and I gave it all I had. I went straight into the lead and I won the race.

Lauda had got off to a poor start and he was back in eleventh place at the end of the first lap. I had a real cushion, but I knew

Lauda fighting back after a poor start at Estoril, 1984 . . .

*. . . I won my seventh and last race of the championship season. But Lauda
snatched second place – and the world title*

how good he was and how good the McLaren was. As the laps ticked by, Niki picked them off one by one until finally, eighteen laps from the line, the pit crew flashed a signal board that said it all: 'Lauda P2'. He was up in second place. I tried to shut it out of my mind and concentrate on winning, but it was difficult.

Niki took the title by half a point.

My consolation was that I had honoured my contract in every respect, that I had done my very best, and that I had notched up seven wins and committed very few mistakes. I had been the fastest driver all season and Niki graciously acknowledges as much in his autobiography when he alludes to me as 'a fast son-of-a-bitch'.

I won my first world championship title the following year.

15 *The long road to the top prize*

The year I won my first world championship proved to be as hectic as it was unpredictable. Or so it seemed to me, particularly after the first four races of the season, which had clearly shown how one's fortunes can vary from one race to the next. Everyone in Formula One has his own tale to tell, but I think it is worthwhile going into my experiences in 1985 in some detail, if only to show how problems which appeared insurmountable at the time reveal themselves in retrospect to be rather mundane.

The 1984 season had been a killer. I had had to dig deep in what had proved to be a vain attempt to beat Lauda, and I was physically drained. A first priority was to get away from it all. I took Anne-Marie and Nicolas off to the sun of Saint Dominique in the company of the Laffite clan. As it proved, this was an ideal place to recharge my batteries.

Marvellous days at the seaside with Anne-Marie and Nicolas

Once I got back, my first obligation was to take part in an extensive PR campaign for Marlboro, a whistle-stop tour that took Niki and myself all over the world, from Scandinavia to Latin America. It was all rather good fun, despite the sameness of the questions you tend to be asked as a racing driver. Niki turned out to be an excellent travel companion – very philosophical, very laid back, very witty and with an occasional tendency to put his foot in it.

One evening we were at a dinner in Buenos Aires when Niki espied a gorgeous lady in the crowd. He described her attributes in rather basic terms. What he didn't realise was that the husband of the young lady in question was sitting at our table. There was much coughing and clearing of throats, and the atmosphere at our table altered perceptibly: there was a distinct chill in the air.

One of the subjects we kept coming back to during interminably long plane journeys was that of the prospects for the championship season ahead. We had been direct rivals throughout the previous season, and the McLaren team had been unstinting in its efforts to ensure that our respective cars were as perfectly matched as possible. This said, the McLaren had not evolved appreciably, whereas our direct competitors in other Formula One marques had been sharpening up their act.

The other marques had acknowledged at the very onset of the 1984 season that the McLaren-TAG-Porsche constellation was well-nigh unbeatable. As a result, they had focused their efforts on gearing up for the subsequent championship season, knowing full well that there have been few instances in modern Formula One history – only Ferrari and Lotus spring to mind – where the same marque has dominated several seasons on the trot. Sooner or later, a team will go off the boil, its motivation will flag, and its potential for victory will be diluted.

For all this, I was determined to look on the bright side, not least because a racing driver has to think that way – there is nothing more counter-productive than simply rolling over and admitting defeat.

All in all, however, the run-up to the first race of the championship was far from encouraging. The Brazilian Grand Prix was scheduled for 7 April. And, by 5 April, the date of the first official practice, all I had had by way of preparation was ten or so laps in the pouring rain at Brands Hatch, prior to my McLaren being taken apart, crated, and shipped off to Rio. I desperately wanted to believe that the car was in good shape, because I knew

John Barnard, until 1987 the creative genius behind the McLaren-MP Series

it would be extremely difficult to make good any ground lost early on in a crowded race calendar.

Friday 5 April saw Niki, myself and the entire McLaren squad hard at work. We had two spanking new mainframes and a third that hadn't even been run in. To be honest, I wasn't looking forward to the next couple of hours.

Practice started at ten o'clock. By eleven, I was in a better frame of mind. Like other MP4s before it, the McLaren MP4–2B was a fine machine. John Barnard had made a whole series of modifications and had radically redesigned the rear suspension. This was particularly successful, because the car coped delightfully with the long, flat and highly technical bends on the Jacarepagua circuit.

Things were looking good.

During practice between 10.00 and 11.30 on Friday or Saturday mornings before a Grand Prix, the top teams all follow the same routine. For the better part of an hour, they monitor the car's performance with varying quantities of fuel on board, check how the car handles with virtually a full tank, and adjust the car's set-up accordingly. They are then ready for the qualifying laps which are driven between one and four o'clock on the Friday or Saturday afternoon, when the car carries as light a fuel load as possible and is set up for optimal speed rather than for actual race conditions.

In Rio, when we were all adjusting and readjusting our basic set-up positions, I seemed to be in good shape. But when it came to qualifying, I couldn't do better than sixth position. It was obvious that the other marques had done a lot of work on their engines and had developed significantly improved boost values. The most notable progress was at Renault and Honda.

At McLaren, there was never any question of Porsche spending time developing an engine exclusively with qualifying in mind. The attitude was that there was no need, as long as you were comparatively well-placed on the starting grid. I must say that I had my doubts about this, but I have to admit that they were right: it made much more sense to concentrate on the engine's performance in the race proper (except in one-off situations like Monaco, where overtaking can be a problem).

I was fastest in the Sunday morning warm-up, when the car had been set up for anticipated race conditions. I had no problem in selecting the appropriate tyre compounds.

What is more, I had no problem in winning.

The lead group comprised three cars – Rosberg's Williams, Alboreto's Ferrari, and my McLaren. Rosberg blew a turbo, leaving Alboreto in the lead with a car that had a top speed superior to mine. But he missed a gear change and I was through. Prost 9 points, Alboreto 6.

It started to rain just before the start of the Portuguese Grand Prix and race conditions changed constantly as the rain grew heavier, eased off, then came on heavy again. The race was a hit-or-miss affair, dodging the puddles and the storm drains.

1985 gets off to a bad start: De Angelis is leading and I am heading for a spin

Senna's Lotus-Renault went off into the lead, shielded by his understudy De Angelis. I clung on behind De Angelis for all of thirty laps, but it was tough going – my engine was not adapting too well to the conditions and I was driving blind because of the spray thrown up by the Lotus. I did my level best to overtake on several occasions, but I eventually went into a double spin and ended up in the guardrail. After the race, Henri Pescarolo – a specialist in the wet – was quoted as saying that I had driven a brilliant race. Maybe so, but the bottom line was Alboreto 12 points, Prost 9.

The San Marino Grand Prix at Imola calls for rapid surges of acceleration and violent braking. Together, these add up to heavy fuel consumption and you really have to keep your wits about you on that score.

I was doing well after several laps, keeping in touch with a breakaway group led by Senna, De Angelis and Alboreto. Then, six laps from the finishing line, I had a signal from the pits to watch my fuel. I eased up and Senna disappeared out of sight. Next thing I knew was Johansson's Ferrari sweeping past me.

Suddenly it was all happening. On the fifty-seventh lap, I saw Senna's Lotus parked on the side of the circuit. A little farther on, I came across Johansson's Ferrari, also parked. Then I flashed across the finishing line in number one spot, ahead of De Angelis.

I was being interviewed after the race and the victory ceremony, when Ron Dennis came up and discreetly tugged at my sleeve. It had been determined that my McLaren was two kilos under regulation weight. I had been disqualified.

Two disappointments in a row after the euphoria of Brazil: the result was De Angelis 16 points, Prost still on 9.

I needed a win and I needed one fast if I was to keep in the running. I got one, thanks to a spectacular shunt involving Piquet and Patrese, both of whom – fortunately – were unhurt.

The venue was Monaco, where Alboreto's Ferrari was beyond any doubt the fastest car in the race.

I had mapped out a prudent plan of attack revolving around the need to take care of my tyres, because I didn't want to come into the pits to change them. Senna and Alboreto were well out in front, and I was in third place, playing a waiting game.

Senna blew his engine early on in the race, leaving Alboreto out on his own. On the seventeenth lap, Piquet and Patrese got tangled up. There were bits of car all over the place and water and oil on the circuit. Alboreto came through, hit some oil, and skidded straight into the run-off zone at Saint Devôte. Luckily for him, his engine didn't cut out and he was able to rejoin the race.

I was now in the lead. I deliberately stuck to my game plan, however, and it was only a matter of time before I saw Alboreto's Ferrari coming up fast in my rear mirror. Six laps later, Michele swept past me back into the lead. This time, however, he didn't seem to be pulling away as fast as he had done earlier on. On the contrary, he was slowing down and, on the thirty-second lap, he pulled into the pits. He had punctured a tyre coming through the debris left by Piquet and Patrese.

Alboreto changed all four tyres and came back into the attack. But it started to rain on the final laps. With my premature exit in 1982 still fresh in my memory, I eased off a little. Michele followed suit. He was well up in the title race and, like myself, he needed a result.

The Alboreto/Ferrari combination was beginning to look ominously good. The Ferraris had undoubtedly come along by leaps and bounds, and I knew Michele of old. Away from the track, he was quiet, restrained, courteous and affable. But on it, he was a fierce and highly-motivated competitor, who would stop at nothing to win. He was going to be a tough adversary.

Meanwhile, De Angelis was still racking up the points: De Angelis 20, Prost 18.

The next race after Monaco was the Belgian Grand Prix. This had been scheduled for Francorchamps, one of my favourite circuits, very fast and with sweeping natural bends. Unfortunately, the newly resurfaced track was in such poor condition that the race wasn't a practical proposition. So we packed our bags and left.

We moved on to North America, to the Canadian Grand Prix in Montreal. This was a circuit where fuel consumption and hard braking are at a premium. Like Detroit, home of the US Grand Prix, Montreal is a black spot on the Grand Prix calendar – an ugly, congested, eminently forgettable circuit.

I came third in Montreal, pipped by the two Ferraris. In Detroit, I drove into the wall during qualifying, injuring my wrist. And, since I couldn't cope with yanking the steering-wheel to full lock and back (which is a necessity in Detroit), I pulled up during the race. Rosberg won in the Williams-Honda.

Alboreto 31 points, Prost 22.

After our detour to North America, we got back to some real and attractive circuits, starting with Paul Ricard.

The TAG-Porsche engine had been progressively modified and my McLaren was in prime condition. I stress the 'my', because Lauda – for some unknown reason – was going through one of the roughest patches of his whole career, plagued by one technical hitch after another.

Piquet and the Brabham-BMW were unbeatable at that French Grand Prix, but I remember the race for another reason, because I went for – and got away with – an unbelievable manoeuvre.

I knew that Rosberg was faster than I was on the straight and that I had the edge in the corners. Needless to say, he knew this too. The only hope was to catch him off guard at the one point on the circuit where he would least expect me to make my move. This was in the 'S' at La Verrerie, a very dangerous bend because you take it at speeds in excess of 165 mph and the line through it is like the eye of a needle.

For a number of laps, I shadowed Rosberg through La Verrerie. Excellent driver that he is, he hit exactly the same spot time after time. There was only a split second to overtake or, to be more accurate, to draw level and oblige him to let me through. I managed to thread that particular needle and, to this day, I am very proud of that manoeuvre at a point where tradition has it that there is, quite simply, nothing on.

Alboreto had been forced to retire. I was making some headway. Alboreto 31 points, Prost 26.

The British Grand Prix was held at Silverstone, one of the fastest circuits in the championship. After trying out in practice, I knew I had to drive with one eye on the fuel gauge and, more important, the other on my tyres, because I had deliberately opted for a softer compound, one of the advantages peculiar to the McLaren.

Senna and I fought out a spectacular duel. I had taken Mansell, De Cesaris and Rosberg, and was behind Senna, shadowing his every move. I challenged for the lead on several occasions at

A l'attaque!

different points on the circuit, but he shut the door every time. I switched tactics to harassment, but he kept his nerve. Suddenly, eight laps from the flag, he cracked. His engine had cut out. I went past him and immediately turned the boost down, but his engine came to life again and he forced himself back into the lead.

I made up my mind to bide my time and save my final, all-out attack for the last lap. It wasn't necessary. He ran out of fuel and I won my third Grand Prix of the season. Alboreto joined me on the podium in third place.

Alboreto 37 points, Prost 35.

Teo Fabi and the Toleman took everybody by surprise by qualifying in pole position on the Friday of the German Grand Prix at Nürburgring, a position he held on to because it rained during qualifying on the Saturday.

I was in third position, which is to say directly behind him on the starting grid. I had every confidence that, all things being equal, Fabi would get away to a good start. But all things were not equal, and I had misgivings about the Hart engine that powered his Toleman. Added to this was the fact that Teo had very kindly come over to me seconds before the start of the race to warn me that his clutch was misbehaving. I told him that, if he had trouble getting away, I would pull out and pass on the left.

As it happened, he got away beautifully, and I was the one who was left at the gate. As a result, I was back in fifth place at the end of the first lap. Alboreto, who had outbraked – and nudged – Johansson in the race to the first corner, was battling it out up front against Rosberg and Senna. Once Rosberg lost speed and Senna retired, Alboreto had a clear field. I was up in second place by this time, but there was nothing I could do to catch him because a turbo collar had detached and I had a broken heat exchanger.

I had lost ten seconds getting away from the grid and I was ten seconds adrift at the finish, despite going into a spin along the way. My engine had let me down, but I was at fault, too.

Alboreto 46, Prost 41.

The Austrian Grand Prix was eventful. During the Sunday morning warm-up, I went off at speed in the chicane at the exact moment you have to hit the accelerator to come out of it. My accelerator pedal jammed and I ploughed straight into one of the many embankments that line the Österreichring at Zeltweg. Manou Zurini, the photographer, was close by and he recalled fearing the worse, because my McLaren was inches away from flipping over.

The car was quickly repaired, but it was never quite right. Nevertheless, I won the race without any great difficulty.

There were two starts to that Grand Prix. The first one resulted in a pile-up which involved Alboreto among others, but he was able to switch to his reserve car for the second start and he eventually finished third. The fits and starts that stand out in my mind are not those, however, but the ones involving Niki Lauda.

For some time now, Niki had been intimating to Ron Dennis that he was keen to call it a day. I believe that was another turning point in my own life, because Niki and I were very close by this time and we had a lot of respect for each other.

Ron had already approached me for my opinion as to who might replace Niki for the 1986 season and I had given him my own 'short list' of drivers who – to my mind – were not only excellent in their own right but also capable of working together for the welfare of the team rather than looking out exclusively for number one. By this I mean that success comes when the whole team pulls together right up to the start of the race, at which point the individual driver has a free hand to do his own thing.

There were four names on my list: Keke Rosberg, Michele Alboreto, Elio de Angelis and Ayrton Senna. (As God is my witness, I hadn't exactly chosen also-rans!) Later, some of the less informed press would report that I had been opposed to Senna, the bright new star on the Grand Prix horizon, because Ron Dennis eventually went for Rosberg. As you can see, the unfounded and malicious rumours were already starting to make the rounds. As discreetly as I could, I pointed out to the rumour-mongers – albeit in the presence of a few witnesses – that, instead of asking me why I didn't want Senna as a stablemate, they would be better advised asking Senna why he couldn't join McLaren. In effect, his various contractual obligations were such that he could not have joined McLaren in 1986 or, for that matter, in 1987.

I do not remember all the details of the hastily-convened press conference in Austria called to announce Lauda's departure and Rosberg's arrival. But, as far as I can make out, Lauda was furious with the offhanded attitude he discerned in Ron Dennis, who simply made the announcement as if Lauda no longer existed. Ron certainly has a number of very considerable talents, but he has his faults – among them an annoying habit of dismissing as being of little consequence anything that he himself hasn't dreamt up, anticipated or decreed.

I had a taste of this in 1988 when the editors of *Autosport*, one of the most widely-read motor racing journals in the United Kingdom, approached me for permission to run a translation of a column I have been writing for some years now in the French magazine *Auto Journal*. *Autosport* had one hell of a time – and so did I – trying to get across to Ron what they wanted. I wasn't giving away any team secrets or other such information in my column, but Ron didn't like it, and that was that. It hadn't been his idea.

Another episode stands out in my mind, also dating from 1988. Having won a number of times at Monaco, I knew Prince Rainier quite well, certainly well enough to know that he was very proper, very dignified and very formal. (In 1981, my mother had come to see me race and had managed to worm her way in without a ticket, by the simple expedient of brandishing her ID card and kicking up a little fuss. Getting into the stands at Monaco without a ticket is quite an achievement, by the way, but my mother has all her wits about her. She may even have bragged a little about it. At all events, Prince Rainier got to hear of her exploit and he mentioned it to me *en passant*. Enough said!)

A certain protocol attaches to winning the Monaco Grand Prix. Tradition has it that Prince Rainier and the winner come into dinner together. In 1988, Ron Dennis was supposed to pick me up and drive me to the gala dinner on the evening after the Grand Prix. Predictably, he was late. It was more or less immaterial to him, because it wasn't *his* banquet. Although I realise that the breach of etiquette was perhaps not all that serious, I detest being embarrassed for next to no reason.

To get back to the Austrian Grand Prix: I had won and I was now lying equal first with Alboreto.

Fifty points each.

We moved on from Austria to the Dutch Grand Prix at Zandvoort. This was one of the very rare occasions when Anne-Marie came along. As a rule, she will only watch races on television, and Zandvoort was only her third 'live' Grand Prix since I had started racing in 1980.

Quite simply speed makes her nervous. I remember once driving her along a road somewhere in France – this was when I was an established Formula One driver – and she got so nervous that she shouted at me, 'Who do you think you are – Fangio?' (This ties in nicely with another anecdote. In 1986, when I was on my way back from the Grand Prix in Pau which I had helped organise, I stopped

Messing about in the Mirage

over in Bordeaux and went up in a Mirage, courtesy of the French Air Force. Back on terra firma, I set off home, only to be caught in a radar trap, doing well in excess of the speed limit. The gendarme looked me up and down disdainfully before asking: 'Who do you think you are – Alain Prost?')

At Zandvoort, I held the lead until I had to come in for a tyre change. One of the wheel bolts jammed and I lost close on twenty seconds in the pits. Lauda took over the lead. I closed up on him and stayed there for the last few laps, but he kept shutting the door on me. And quite right, too. He had nothing to lose and I had everything to gain.

It turned out that Alboreto could place no higher than fourth. So, for the first time since the Brazilian Grand Prix, I was in the lead in the championship. Alboreto 53 points, Prost 56.

The Italian Grand Prix at Monza was plain sailing. I was lying second behind Keke Rosberg's Williams and I was in Alboreto's slipstream ready to lap him. Suddenly, Rosberg pulled up, his engine blown, and, one lap later, I saw my pit man Ben flash a jubilant 'Albo out', meaning that the Ferrari had gone too. I had opened up a gap.

Alboreto 53 points, Prost 65.

We went back again to Spa-Francorchamps in Belgium to discover that, this time, the circuit was usable. It was raining, however, and the surface was dicey, so the watchword was caution.

I finished third, posting the fastest lap time of the day. With the title at stake, I was furious at having had to decline to mix it with Senna and Nigel Mansell, who battled all the way to the line. Still, I was now sixteen points ahead of Alboreto.

I didn't need a slide-rule to work out the situation. There were three more Grand Prix left in the championship: the European Grand Prix at Brands Hatch, the South African and the Australian. I could take the title at Brands, provided I could somehow edge two further points clear of Alboreto. And I was desperate to do just that, because I already knew how agonising it could be to wait out the very last races of a season, when self-doubt starts to grip you like a vice.

Two points, I kept reminding myself. Two points. And all manner of permutations. The top six finishers are awarded nine, six, four,

Brands Hatch, 1985: a few words of encouragement from Laffite before the start of the race

three, two and one respectively. I could do it in so many different ways.

They do say that the hardest way is the best.

When you are within shouting distance of a world championship, you tend to lose perspective. What might otherwise be dismissed as trivial suddenly assumes monumental proportions.

From where I was sitting, the 1985 European Grand Prix at Brands started off as a disaster. You would hardly credit it: Rosberg, who had never been stranded on the grid in his entire career, froze in front of me when the green light came on. I had made my mind up to drive 'normally', that is not too cautiously and not too aggressively. And here I was, a quarter of a second into the race, and I was churning up the grass trying to avoid Rosberg.

Rosberg finally got going. I slammed on opposite lock to extricate myself from the greenery and inched back onto the circuit, keeping my fingers crossed that the pack wouldn't slam into me. They roared by, hugging the ground.

To be sure of beating Alboreto, I had to place in the first five. And here I was, fourteenth at the end of the first lap. I was livid. I simply couldn't believe it. The only time I really had to get away cleanly, and I'd blown it.

There was no point in crying over spilt milk. My only option was to keep going.

Lap two, in twelfth place, Alboreto running eighth.

Lap seven, seventh. Alboreto sixth, and in the points.

Lap nine, sixth, and in the points. Alboreto seventh, out of the points.

And so on. Ahead of me, De Angelis, Johansson and Watson (standing in for Lauda, who had damaged his wrist at Spa-Francorchamps) were locked in a titanic struggle, and I didn't relish getting caught up amongst that trio, all the more so because my McLaren didn't appear to be handling too well.

Then I caught a first glimpse of blue in my rear-view mirror. Jacques Laffite was gaining on me fast. That was a body blow. Jacques, who had come over to wish me luck on the grid, was driving his own race; it was his job to take me if he could and mine to move over if he had the edge.

Lap eighteen: Jacques made his move. He pushed me back into seventh place again, out of the points. But I had just seen a welcome sight – a huge cloud of white smoke belching out of Alboreto's Ferrari.

Brands Hatch, 1985: Alboreto blows his engine

Lap thirty-eight. Halfway. I came in for a tyre change and Ron Dennis put on the softest compound he had. That's why the car had been handling badly up to now – the tyres were too hard.

Lap thirty-nine: eighth.

Lap forty-two: Brundle pulled out. I am lying seventh.

Lap fifty-two: Laffite changed tyres. I was lying sixth now, back in the points yet again.

Lap fifty-six: Johansson retired and I passed De Angelis. Up into fourth place.

I squeezed past Rosberg into third, but he came back at me and I let him through again. Fourth place is enough. Just stay in fourth place to the flag. That is all I had to do.

I accelerated into Clearways for the last time.

The chequered flag came down.

Words of comfort for Alboreto from his friend Ghinzani. 1985 was not to be his year

It was 6 October 1985. I was world champion, the first French world champion in the history of Formula One.

As far as I know, I didn't gesticulate wildly. I do recollect that my eyes misted over behind my visor. This was *my* moment, a very private moment of sheer joy that was mine alone, not yet shared with my family or any of those who had helped me along the way.

After that, it was champagne in the cockpit, then up onto the podium. Four steps this time, the top one reserved for the world champion.

We celebrated into the small hours . . . .

16 *Friendship and rivalry*

The morning after.

I knew that 6 October 1985 would be one day in my life that I would never forget. But it was essential to put Brands Hatch and the European Grand Prix behind me, because there was still a lot of the season left.

First of all, we were off to Kyalami for what turned out to be the last South African Grand Prix of recent years. The final stop was Australia, where the citizens of Adelaide were girding their loins for their first-ever Formula One world championship event.

I was very keen to visit Australia again, because it is so far removed – in every sense of the term – from Europe and its preoccupations, indeed, from the Western world as a whole. It was my second trip down under: I had the good fortune to take part in – and win – a Formula Pacific event in Australia back in 1982.

The Australians gave me a champion's welcome, but that isn't why I have so much affection for their country. What I like about Australia is the variety of scenery, regions and climates. And I also like the Aussie character, which I would generalise as having all the good features of the English and none of their failings. The Australians are very tough and level-headed, but they also have an easy-going charm about them – all of which makes for an attractive quality of life.

Since then, I have been back to Australia three times – in 1986, 1987 and 1988 – and I have seen enough of the place to think of buying a house there. In a word, I enjoy being there.

En route to Adelaide, Anne-Marie and I stopped over in Rome to visit the Vatican. I had promised myself that, if I won the world championship, I would seek an audience with the Pope, because I was very impressed by his overall personality and his clarity of thought and expression. I brought him a present for his personal collection. The fact that I was granted an audience seemed to astonish all and sundry. What? Prost was a believer? Yes, I certainly am and I have never concealed the fact.

Once I got back from Adelaide I had to honour a few commitments which I had been unable to attend to immediately after Brands Hatch. In essence, these were engagements and personal appearances arranged in honour of the new world champion. I don't recall in any great detail all the dinners and receptions I attended, but there are two occasions which stand out in my memory.

One was a delightful evening among friends in my home town of Saint Chamond, which had just built a gymnasium complex bearing my name. The other was much more formal, but nonetheless moving. This was when French President François Mitterrand conferred on me the *Légion d'Honneur*.

Among the other recipients of that honour were a couple of people I knew rather well – Jacques Laffite, for one, and Jean Todt, of Peugeot. I was to meet President Mitterrand again a short while afterwards, at a less formal and rather protracted breakfast organised by one of his advisers, Jean Glavany, who is a motor racing fanatic. Jacques was there too, as was Jean Todt, for whom I have great respect and with whom I subsequently developed a much closer relationship. It is hard to imagine anyone more passionately committed to motor sport than Jean, so we certainly had a lot in common right from the start. But there is more to it than that. I have come to appreciate his acute perception, his instinctive grasp of what makes motor sport tick, his empathy with the drivers, and the intellectual honesty he brings to bear as head of Peugeot's competition division; it is hard to find fault with him.

At the professional level, my dealings with Jean Todt go back a long way. In fact, if he had received the go-ahead to establish a Peugeot Formula One team, I might very well have been his first driver. As of today, however, his plans in that direction have not materialised. In any case, we are still firm friends.

At the end of 1986, when I took the world championship for the second time, I took part in a parade down the Champs Elysées. I was in my McLaren, flanked by the two Finnish rally drivers and the two Peugeot 205 Turbo 16s that had been instrumental in winning a second world title for Jean Todt and Peugeot. It was a beautiful way to pay tribute to two French champions.

There was a break of nearly five-and-a-half months between the final race of the 1985 season in Adelaide and the first race of the

1986 season in Brazil. But that shouldn't be taken to mean that I didn't do my share of driving during that period. True, my vacation was a little bit longer than usual, but there was a series of private test drives for McLaren, not to mention the preliminary tests organised by FOCA immediately prior to the Brazilian Grand Prix.

I took stock of my prospects for the 1986 season, due to open in Rio in a few days time. I had had plenty of time to analyse the different factors which would have an impact on the forthcoming world championship. But there were still a number of unknowns.

Who would be our closest challengers? During practice in Rio, three cars and three drivers seemed particularly impressive: Piquet and Mansell in the Williams-Honda, and Senna in the Lotus-Renault. It seemed to me that the Williams team was probably the pick of the crop that year for a number of reasons: a new chassis developed by Patrick Head, one of the sharpest designers in the business; the sheer professionalism of the squad, even though Frank Williams himself had been seriously injured in a road accident and

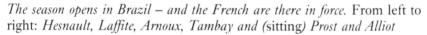

The season opens in Brazil – and the French are there in force. From left to right: *Hesnault, Laffite, Arnoux, Tambay and (sitting) Prost and Alliot*

99

*The 'Gang of Four'. Between us, we won every Grand Prix of the 1986
championship season.* From left to right: *Senna, Prost, Mansell and Piquet.
With those three around, winning wasn't easy . . .*

was paralysed; and, not least, because we all knew that Japan's
Honda was prepared to invest vast sums of money to underwrite a
title-winning Formula One racing engine.

However, if there was one question mark against the Williams,
it had to be with regard to the Honda engine. The international
federation, still committed to curbing excessive power, had already
announced that Formula One tanks could now hold a maximum of
195 litres of racing fuel. In Rio, Mansell had tried out for distance,
driving the equivalent of a full Grand Prix. Williams had scheduled
sixty-two laps – one starting lap followed by sixty-one laps of the
circuit, as tradition demands in Brazil. Mansell had run out of fuel
on lap sixty . . . .

After the two Williams, I identified Senna and his Lotus-Renault
as a force to be reckoned with, but I had certain reservations.
During the close season, there had been speculation that all was
not rosy between Senna and Lotus. Lotus had made a move to take
on Derek Warwick as Senna's teammate, but Senna allegedly

would have none of it. It was said that he was totally opposed to Lotus hiring another top-name driver, because he didn't feel Lotus had the resources to race with two first-rank drivers and he wanted the entire team effort to be committed to himself.

If that was the case, then – to my mind – he was wrong. It is always better to have two good drivers rather than a single driver if you want to develop and refine a car's performance. At the same time, I was favourably impressed by Renault's new engine, even though the company was in the process of pulling out of Formula One as a team and restricting itself to supplying engines to individual marques.

The engine Renault unveiled at the Brazilian Grand Prix was something special. It wasn't until some three months later, in Montreal, that I realised just what Renault had been up to during qualifying earlier in the season.

All supercharged engines are equipped with waste-gates to mitigate the effects of mounting exhaust gas pressure accumulating in the system. Once this pressure reaches a certain level, it will blow the engine. This is where the waste-gate comes in: at a pre-set pressure level, a valve opens and the exhaust gases are released, easing the pressure and thereby preserving the life of the engine. When it came to qualification, Renault had boosted the engine's performance by the simple expedient of removing the two waste-gates and blocking their outlets. The result was that the engine was allowed to build up colossal pressure during the three-lap qualifying period (one lap to come up to speed, one lap qualifying *per se*, and a final, slower lap back into the pits). And the Renault engine was so resilient that it didn't even splutter, let alone blow.

That Saturday in Montreal, I proposed to Ron Dennis that we use the same stratagem. He laughed like a drain. No way. I persisted and he finally gave me the go-ahead, albeit with one small condition attached: 'O.K. But if you blow the engine, you have to buy another one from Porsche. It's coming out of your wages.' That was fine by me. We removed the waste-gate.

Halfway through my first lap the engine blew.

That tells you how powerful and reliable the new Renault engine was.

How did McLaren measure up to Williams and Lotus?

I knew that I was in good shape, both physically and mentally. Winning your first world championship is a bit like winning your first Grand Prix – you have given your all for weeks, months, even years, then suddenly everything falls into place, you've done it, and you start to believe that you are every bit as capable as your predecessors, maybe even more so. For this reason, if for no other, I was highly motivated.

Over at Porsche, Hans Mezger was still in charge of the TAG project and his people had been very busy. They had a number of technical tricks up their sleeve. They were even contemplating changing their turbo supplier of many years' standing, KKK – a clear indication that they were pulling out all the stops in a bid to retain the title.

At this point, I hadn't really test-driven the new McLaren MP4-2C designed by John Barnard and his team. All I knew was based on twenty-five miles or so in heavy rain at Brands Hatch, running-in the chassis before the team all took off for Rio. Like this time last year, we weren't ready. (On the other hand, a quick pre-season drive in the rain at Brands had turned out quite well for me in 1985. Was this a good omen?)

There was one other unknown quantity, and a big one at that: Rosberg. I would have to wait and see. As the season progressed, Keke showed himself in his true light as a great guy, but I had one or two reservations early on.

He had arrived at McLaren fully conscious of his ability and reputation. He wasn't simply any old driver who would have given an arm and a leg to get into one of the top teams. Many are called, but few are chosen. He made this pretty obvious in Rio, when he was introduced to the car for the first time. In retrospect, it was quite amusing but, at the time, I was flabbergasted.

Keke levered himself into the cockpit and John Barnard suggested he do a quick lap just to get the feel of things, then come back into the pits so that the cockpit could be tailored to his physical requirements. Rosberg seemed to be listening with half an ear. He took off, drove a first lap and then, instead of coming back in, he put his foot down and drove a second lap all out. John Barnard's eyes glazed over. Ron Dennis was thunderstruck. At McLaren, you think long and hard before disregarding John's valuable and steely-eyed counsel.

From the pits in Rio, you can see a fair section of the circuit, not least the long straight below the main stands, which leads into a majestic left-hander where you have to apply the brakes exceedingly carefully. We could hear Rosberg gunning the McLaren close to the limit, oblivious to Barnard's instructions. He flashed down the straight, at virtually maximum revs, and disappeared into the bend in an enormous mushroom cloud of dust. Not only had he left the track, he had demolished the car. The show was over. I doubt if John Barnard and he ever saw genuinely eye to eye after that.

A short while before the Brazilian Grand Prix, it was Formula One week in Sestriere. Each year, this delightful Italian mountain resort plays host to Formula One drivers and their families, who spend a week relaxing and indulging in winter sports. The odd journalist or two is also invited. Inevitably, conversation came round to the new McLaren – extensively modified, with a lower centre of gravity, and a six-speed box like the Williams and the Ferrari – and to Rosberg.

As usual, I was very frank. I said that he had made a very favourable impression: he was very aggressive, he was very skilful, and he was hungry. My feeling was that he would be a better qualifier than myself, but I also sensed that I might hold an ace or two under race conditions, because I knew the McLaren inside out and I recognised that it had to be driven with a certain degree of finesse, which was not exactly Keke's long suit at the time. All in all, I reasoned that I would have to play a tactical game, avoiding too many risks and preparing each race in even more minute detail than in the past. At the same time, I would have to take my chances as and when they arose, never pass up an opportunity to win, but – equally – never throw caution to the winds.

In Rio, Piquet benefitted from a first-lap *contretemps* between Senna and Mansell to drive to an uncontested win. Substandard fuel combined with a fault in the computer system to blow my engine – and Rosberg's. In Spain, Senna took the flag a hair's breadth ahead of Mansell, and I had to settle for third. In my anxiety to watch my fuel consumption and save my tyres, I had driven too far within myself. Not a good result.

However, my pre-season diagnosis had been vindicated: the Williams-Honda and the Lotus-Renault were the strongest marques.

The McLaren seemed to be in with a chance in the San Marino Grand Prix at Imola. The car was well suited to the circuit there. Although I had failed to finish in Rio, I had driven the fastest warm-up lap over a similar sort of circuit.

In Imola, fuel consumption is the be-all and end-all. Coming into the race, I tried out two turbo permutations – large turbos, synonymous with power but heavy on fuel, and smaller turbos, which are more versatile and, above all, relatively fuel-efficient. I took the precaution of driving two test laps with two different cars, but I didn't come down on one side or the other until a few minutes before the race. Large or small?

I finally opted for the smaller turbos; Rosberg went the other way. The two McLarens swept all before them until Rosberg ran out of fuel two laps from the line. My own engine started to cough on the last lap, but I shook the car around to extract the last drop of fuel. I came to a standstill just beyond the line.

I had lived up to the number one emblazoned on my car, denoting the reigning world champion.

That win at Imola, in the third race of the championship season, was an important one, because it put the zest back into the McLaren team. We went on to Monaco, where I was every bit as scrupulous in my preparation as I had been in Imola. I secured pole position, took the lead right away and held it without difficulty through to the finish. One other thing: I set the car up for comfort rather than for optimal technical performance, because Monaco is a very exhausting drive. It paid off.

That second win of the season in Monaco put me in the lead in the world championship, ahead of Senna and Piquet. But I knew that after the next Grand Prix, the Belgian, I would scarcely have time to catch my breath, because all the subsequent races followed in rapid succession.

There were frustrations ahead. In Belgium, I had every prospect of winning, but a shunt at the start of the race meant that I only finished sixth. Berger got away too slowly and I was caught between his Benetton and the crash barrier, only to be squeezed by Senna a few metres further on, with no option but to drive into him.

There were amusing moments, too. During a press conference after the Canadian Grand Prix, I was demonstrating how I had outbraked someone or other when my chair skidded. I did a backward roll and disappeared from view under the dais, to the amusement and sympathetic applause of the assembled US and Canadian press.

In Detroit, I hit the wall slap bang in front of the pits. I was disgusted at having dropped a clanger like that in full view of the stands and I scuttled off as soon as I decently could to hide my shame. I went up to Laffite's hotel room, where he and some friends were glued to a TV set watching France play Brazil in the 1986 World Cup. Jacques was beside himself, ranting, raving, leaping up and down, banging his head against the walls. And every now and then, there would be a call from Gérard Larrousse to remind him that he was supposed to be at a team briefing in one of the other rooms in the hotel. Jacques finally relented and went along to the briefing. However, as soon as he got there, he was back on the telephone to us and we had to give him a blow-by-blow account of every subsequent phase of the match. He had me in stitches.

I suspect that Jacques' relationship with Gérard Larrousse was somewhat fragile; whether that was true or not, his behaviour that day certainly didn't help matters.

When I got back to my car the following day, there was a little scrap of paper scotchtaped to the windscreen. This is standard procedure, and normally serves to remind the driver that new brake discs have been mounted or that a fresh gearbox has to be nursed. In this way, the head mechanic can alert the driver to important details he should look out for during practice. The scrap of paper had the following message: 'Differential, brakes, wishbone upper left, wishbone upper right, steering, suspension, gearbox, engine, heat exchanger, underbody, wings – all new. Three hours sleep.' That was the damage I'd done the day before in the chicane.

Amusing little episodes like these play an important part in the life of a Formula One driver to the extent that they help distract you, if only momentarily, from much more serious issues, like the shunt which killed Elio de Angelis while he was on a private test drive at Paul Ricard. It happened in the treacherous 'S' bend at La Verrerie – where I had also had a couple of anxious moments. The probable cause was a ruptured rear wing support, or so we are told. I wasn't far behind him at the time. All I saw was a quick burst of flame. Alan Jones and I were the first to stop, but there was nothing we could do.

Elio was a true gentleman. He had style. On very rare occasions, at a special dinner, he would smoke a cigarette or have a glass of excellent wine. When his friends pointed out that he was smoking and drinking, he would reply that those were some of the *other* good things in life. He was right. I'll never forget him during the drivers' strike in Kyalami, sitting there at the piano. He was an artist.

Then Jacques came a cropper at Brands Hatch at the start of the British Grand Prix. He was in his one hundred and seventy-sixth Grand Prix that day, equalling Graham Hill's Formula One record. It took some minutes – they seemed like hours – to cut him free of the car. He was in a mess, with broken legs, ankles, heels

105

and pelvis. I went with him as far as the ambulance. The pain was so terrible that he blacked out. I was shattered. I had never felt so low. I went to the hospital a few hours later. His wife Bernadette was there at the bedside, together with Pierre Landereau, one of his oldest friends. Jacques was incredibly brave, but he was going through agony. I was trembling all over, because I am afraid of pain.

I am happy to say that even an old warhorse like Jacques can't be put out to pasture before his time. He is no longer in Formula One, but he now competes in touring car events as BMW's works driver. His experience at Brands threw me completely and there was no way I could drive a decent race. Still, my problems were infinitely less serious than his.

Back in the championship, we had moved on to Germany and then to Hungary. I was building up my leg muscles: in Germany, I had to push the McLaren the last few hundred metres to the line after running out of fuel. In Hungary, it was a long hike back to the pits. I seemed to be having more than my fair share of mechanical problems and, to cap it all, I had collided with Arnoux.

Arnoux came over at the end of the race to offer his apologies. That was very nice of him. Actually, he had motioned me through, but I was so surprised that I simply rear-ended him. René added that, in his view, the whole race had been a piece of crap.

I could only agree. The organisers in Budapest had done their level best to put together this first Hungarian Grand Prix, but they really have to be taken to task for not staking out a more attractive course with the funds at their disposal. I remember making my journalist friend Johnny Rives smile by telling him, in all seriousness, that Jerez and Budapest weren't race circuits at all.

The Automobile Club of Hungary had planned a special event to coincide with the Grand Prix. This was the official unveiling of a plaque to commemorate a great Hungarian driver, Ferenc Sziz, who had driven for Renault in the early part of this century and who had won the 1906 French Grand Prix, the only Grand Prix raced that year. As director of Renault-Sport, my old friend Jean Sage had been invited to attend the ceremony and observe the traditional one minute's silence. He asked me to join him as a gesture of courtesy to our Hungarian hosts.

I cut short a briefing at McLaren and dashed over to the main hall attached to the circuit, where the memorial plaque had been erected. The inscription confirmed that Sziz had won the French

Above: *British Grand Prix, Brands Hatch, 1986 – Rosberg leading me into Paddock Bend*

Left: *I won my second world championship in 1986*

Grand Prix held on 26 and 27 June, 1906. 'Two days?' I whispered to Jean. 'Yes, my friend,' he replied with a smile, 'in those days a Grand Prix *was* a Grand Prix, not one of those silly little races you youngsters are involved in today. The 1906 French Grand Prix was 1,230 kilometres long.'

The 1986 Hungarian Grand Prix was the eleventh race of the season. There were only five races left, and nothing had gone right ever since the French Grand Prix or, frankly, since my victory in Monaco. That went for both on the track and off it.

In July, I made a discreet trip to Japan for talks with the Formula One people at Honda. Ron Dennis was looking to replace the Porsche engine at an early date. Negotiations were at a relatively advanced stage, and I believe that Honda were all set to let us have their engines. Ron Dennis actually had a contract on his desk when he announced that he felt obliged to check with his lawyers. The Japanese do things differently, and there was one fly in the ointment: Lotus would be getting the Honda engine for the following season, and so would Williams.

Meanwhile, for some reason or other, Ron Dennis and John Barnard were not on the best of terms. Whatever the reason, on the day after the Austrian Grand Prix, John was invited to pack his bags and vacate the premises. He went straight from Woking to Ferrari, his new employers. Ron had also had talks with Renault, but he was anxious not to let go of Porsche in case he ended up with no engine at all. Rumours and speculation were rife.

The only consolation was that things didn't seem to be going too well over at Williams either. Although Mansell had signed on as number two driver, he was making life difficult for Piquet, and certain members of the Williams squad were allegedly aiding and abetting him, all the more so because he was a British driver in a team that is very British indeed. According to those closest to him, Nelson had just about had enough. Things came to a head at Brands Hatch, when Mansell shut the door on his team-mate.

It has to be said that Nigel was in the lead in the world championship table immediately after the Hungarian Grand Prix – he was on 55 points, I was on 53, Senna was on 48, and Piquet on 47. Clearly, Mansell was having a very good season and, equally clearly, the situation was distinctly unpalatable to Piquet. My own selfish view was that their goings-on could very well work to my advantage. The final races of the season were going to be interesting.

Before that, however, a word about the Austrian Grand Prix, where I had one of my rare disagreements with John Barnard.

Keke and I had decided to work together to get the best out of the cars. (Unlike Mansell and Piquet, we never seemed to have any problem getting along.) It was decided that he would try out all the traditional settings and I would experiment with some new ones. John Barnard, meanwhile, had come up with a proposal to mount a smaller skidplate, along the lines of the one used on the Lotus. The chassis of my McLaren was dropped as far as it could go.

The results were singularly disappointing. Not only did we fail to achieve a better performance from the car, we also made it very uncomfortable to drive. At Zeltweg, it was a real bitch. It bucked and kicked every time I hit the slightest bump on the circuit. I hate driving a car which behaves like that, although there are some drivers who can get used to it. I really felt I was torturing the McLaren, and I had too much respect for a fine piece of machinery to do that.

John stuck to his guns, seemingly deaf to my comments. (He can be very obstinate. A week before, in Hungary, he had pulled something similar by refusing to mount downward diffusors on the rear air extractor. That would have improved the car's performance, but he was against it, probably because he hadn't come up with the idea himself.)

To cut a long story short: during warm-up immediately before the Austrian Grand Prix, I decided that there had been more than enough beating around the bush. So I closeted myself for a couple of hours with Tim Wright, who looks after my McLaren, and we set the car up in a classic manner, approximating to the settings being used by Rosberg. We had some very clear benchmarks, but we were still playing it by ear.

As things turned out, Tim and I got it right and the car behaved perfectly, except for the last lap or two, but that was because of something else. For months, we had been plagued by a mysterious malfunction that we couldn't rectify. From time to time, invariably towards the end of a race, the engine would cut out – usually during braking – and then cut back in again. The same problem occurred in Austria, but I was far enough in the lead to make it to the line, although I had a devil of a job to ensure that brakes, gearbox, accelerator and electric pumps all kept functioning.

The Italian Grand Prix came and went, and I came home empty-handed. I had been disqualified for switching to the reserve car at

McLaren engineer Tim Wright

the very last moment because an alternator had shorted out on my
own McLaren. At any rate, I wouldn't have won or even been in
the points. Just as they waved the black flag to indicate my
disqualification, my engine blew. You don't get much more
conclusive than that.

When I got out of the car, I pointed out that I had been allowed
to risk my neck for nothing for all of thirty laps. That seemed idiotic
to me, and I said as much. This was immediately transposed and
reported as 'the race officials' decisions are idiotic,' and I was on
the receiving end of a $5,000 fine. A few days later, a letter came
into McLaren addressed to me. It was from a young English girl,
who clearly felt I was in need of comforting. She enclosed a five-
pound note to help me pay my fine. It was a very nice gesture, so I
sent back the note with an appropriate dedication, and threw in
another fiver to make sure she wasn't out of pocket.

After Italy, Mansell was still leading the championship. He was
now on 61 points, five ahead of Piquet, who had come back strongly.
I had 53 points and Senna 48. The title was sure to go to one of
the four of us, because Rosberg was lying fifth with a mere 22
points. The Portuguese Grand Prix was going to be critical for the
Gang of Four, as the media had promptly taken to calling us.

I wasn't in the best frame of mind to race in Portugal. My brother

Daniel had just died of cancer, and I couldn't stop thinking about him, his family, his little girl (my niece), and my parents, who had taken it very hard and who were perhaps not all that strong themselves. I went down to the circuit only when it was absolutely essential, and I spent the rest of the time indoors with my friends Gilles, Johnny and Jean-Louis, who took care of me without asking too many questions.

Mansell led from start to finish, Piquet spun out trying to come to terms with Senna, and Senna himself ran out of fuel, leaving me to inherit a useful and utterly unexpected second place. At a stroke, Senna was out of the running. The Gang of Four was now the Gang of Three – Mansell, Piquet and myself.

There were only two races left, the Mexican Grand Prix and the Australian Grand Prix.

Mexico dealt Williams a body blow. Berger won in the Benetton, his first Formula One victory. Tyres played a determinant role: Gerhard was on Pirellis and he didn't have to come in for a tyre change. I did, as did Mansell and Piquet.

Coming up to the final race in Australia, there had been a slight change in the rankings. I had squeezed in between Mansell and Piquet. Any one of us could still win, but the advantage was still with Nigel, because he remained in the lead.

Nevertheless, I was still confident, although I realised that it wouldn't be easy. To take the title I absolutely had to win the race, and Mansell had to finish out of the points. Piquet was marginally less of a threat: all I had to do was finish in front of him. My confidence may seem unwarranted. But I knew that I wasn't all alone against Mansell. For a start, Rosberg was on hand to help prevent Mansell winning – Keke had said that he would race for me and he is a man of his word. What is more, there was Piquet. He and Mansell were at daggers drawn.

What also counted for me was the fact that Mansell was going for his first world title, and I could readily imagine the pressures on him. I would never be in that pressure situation again, and neither would Piquet. Before the race, I remember a lot of people expressing amazement at my line of reasoning. The main thing was that I believed in it.

Anne-Marie had decided to come with me to Adelaide. We were given a tremendously warm welcome, just like the year before. Practice went well and I paid particular attention to my tyres. That was something you had to get scrupulously right. On the Saturday afternoon, I was introduced to Mr Honda in person, who no doubt was intrigued to meet this little Frenchman who was making life difficult for his cars.

To take my mind off what was at stake, I needed some distraction on the evening before the race. We had a huge suite at the Adelaide Hilton, with a sitting-room which we shared with Ron Dennis. Anne-Marie was watching television and I was playing a few hands of *belote* with Gilles, Johnny and Jean-Louis. Ron Dennis strolled in. 'Too many Frenchmen in here for my liking,' he said and beat a hasty retreat.

I got into bed at eleven or so, and promptly fell asleep. As a rule, I sleep much less than some of the other drivers, notably Laffite or Piquet, but I always sleep like a log before a race. By contrast, I am always edgy after a race and sleep badly. Lauda was a bit like that, and he would sometimes have a whisky in a bar or nightclub on Sunday evenings after a race to make sure that he got a good night's rest. Be that as it may, the night before the Australian Grand Prix was unexpectedly hectic – the fire alarm went off and everybody had to gather downstairs in the foyer, standing around in various states of undress, chatting to the firemen.

I remember every single detail of the race next day, enough to fill all the pages of this book.

Piquet took an early lead, then Rosberg went past him into first position. I was tucked in so tightly behind Piquet that he finally spun out. I was up in second position behind Rosberg when I caught a kerb, punctured my right front tyre and nearly made a hasty exit. That puncture was to prove crucial, and although I didn't think so at the time, it was a stroke of good fortune.

I now had some ground to make up on Rosberg, Piquet and Mansell. I was lying fourth and we hadn't even reached the halfway stage. The two Williams were battling it out, no holds barred. Taking both of them would be a tough proposition.

I was snapping at Mansell's heels for a time, but he held me off skilfully, so I decided to change tactics. I held well back until we were on the sixty-third lap, less than twenty laps from the finish, then I rocketed out of a corner and came back at him with a vengeance.

It was very, very close. Just as I pulled level with the Williams, I saw Rosberg, who had been hidden by Mansell's car. Not Rosberg's McLaren, but Keke himself, standing at the side of the circuit looking at his car. He got out of the way of me just in time by leaping behind his McLaren. I was committed: I nudged over towards Mansell, forcing him wide and leaving a gap for myself to pull ahead. As all this was happening, I caught a glimpse of Keke shrugging an apology, as if to say, I did my utmost to help out. At the time, he thought he had lost his rear wing. In fact, he had shredded a tyre.

That was where my own puncture before halfway suddenly assumed a whole new relevance. Once they had looked my tyres over in the pits, the Goodyear people had breathed a sigh of relief. They were still convinced that the others, Mansell and Piquet included, would make it to the finish without a tyre change. But Rosberg had just shredded a tyre . . . .

Panic stations. Mansell was called into the pits, but he never made it. A tyre blew and he barely survived an absolutely spectacular exit into the run-out area.

Mansell was out, and the first part of my 'plan' had materialised. But Piquet was still there, and he wouldn't budge. I couldn't blame him for that, because he was in the lead. But he was still on his original set of tyres, whereas I had been in for a change. It was only a matter of time before he was forced to make a pit stop.

To be honest, I must admit that, when he did, I was on my last legs. Fuel consumption was a critical factor in this race, and I had been so preoccupied that I hadn't been able to husband my resources. My fuel gauge showed zero a full two laps before the end of the race. Piquet went for broke. He did everything imaginable to close the gap, but I crossed the finishing line with four seconds in hand.

Four seconds. The longest four seconds of my life. And I erupted with pure joy. I was world champion for the second time.

Next morning, as Anne-Marie and I were going down to breakfast, we saw morning newspapers outside each bedroom all the way along the hotel corridor, with banner headlines proclaiming 'Prost Wins Adelaide Thriller'. And there was a photograph of yours truly, beside the McLaren, dancing for joy.

It was fantastic.

A few months later we were all on vacation in Sestriere for the traditional Formula One week. Someone asked Piquet who he thought was the best driver in the world. His answer: 'All I can say is that, last year, Mansell and I had incontestably the best two cars going. But there was a little French guy with a broken nose, who really took us apart.'

17 *All change at McLaren*

Immediately after the Australian Grand Prix I went off on a long and genuine vacation. No steering wheel, no Formula One, no receptions, no interviews. All I wanted was to spend some time with my family and close friends.

My resolve cracked on only one occasion, when I appeared as guest of honour on Jacques Chancel's TV show, *Le Grand Echiquier*, a Channel 2 spectacular which was marvellous fun. That evening lasted into the small hours, because Mansour Ojjeh had taken over a Paris restaurant for a late supper after the programme to celebrate my second world championship title.

When I recovered, I headed back to Meribel, my favourite ski resort (so much so, that I am in the process of buying a chalet there). Skiing is not exactly an ideal pastime for Formula One drivers but, what the hell, I enjoy it.

As the weeks wore on, however, I had to come back down to earth. Formula One was cranking up for another season and I had to get myself into shape.

Year-end 1986 marked a turning point in the fortunes of the McLaren team. Now that John Barnard had left to join Ferrari, Ron Dennis was running the whole show on his own, and he had to start restructuring the squad. Added to this was the fact that he was putting the finishing touches to a brand new factory in Woking which would act as headquarters for the entire McLaren operation.

The new plant is huge, superbly equipped and, above all else, functional. You have the feeling right away that it has been designed to provide optimal working conditions. In addition to the workshops and research units, it boasts a conference room, restaurants and even a small theatre − presumably to celebrate future triumphs. As you might expect, information technology predominates: sophisticated data-processing systems link every office, workshop and warehouse facility, to the point where each

A living legend in Formula One: Juan-Manuel Fangio, who still drops in on the occasional Grand Prix

engineer can design and immediately test a new element without leaving his own desk. This is true functionalism, a high-tech internal communications system which promotes action and reaction, absolutely essential to a Formula One operation.

Clearly, one of Ron Dennis's priorities was to find a replacement for John Barnard. In doing so, he demonstrated – to my mind, at least – just how far-sighted he can be. First of all, he hired Gordon Murray as technical director, then Neil Oatley as an additional engineer. But he didn't put Murray in charge of developing the new car. Instead, he solicited technical inputs from the McLaren staff as a whole before deciding what the 1987 car would look like.

Ron was to do exactly the same thing in 1988. Steve Nichols was the man behind what was to be the first McLaren-Honda, but every single one of the other engineers – Tim Wright, Gordon Murray, Neil Oatley – made specific contributions. This is one of Ron Dennis's strong points. He is a wizard at getting the most out of a communal effort, preferring this approach to entrusting the entire project to one individual, as the other teams do at present.

Up to this point, I had only had a passing acquaintance with Gordon. To be honest, his eccentricity worried me a little. He was a thorough-going Formula One freak, what with his garish T-shirts, John Lennon glasses and obsession with all things French, including *grand cru* clarets. He had quit his job as technical director over at Brabham, where he had been responsible for a number of innovative design features: he had been deeply affected by the death of Elio de Angelis, the only driver who had died in one of his Formula One designs.

It took some time to get to know Gordon better. What I now like most about him is his intellectual commitment and, above all perhaps, his acute sense of perception.

Neil Oatley is a withdrawn sort of person, probably because he is very shy. Before joining McLaren, he had worked for the FORCE Lola team which Alan Jones and Patrick Tambay had driven for in 1986. Jacques Laffite, who had had Neil as his engineer over at Williams, once asked me if there wouldn't be problems of communication between Neil and myself, because of Neil's excessive shyness. Obviously, no such problems materialised, but that's Jacques for you – he has no equal when it comes to putting your mind at rest.

John Barnard's departure had left Ron Dennis in something of a predicament. There was no way that McLaren's technicians could simply sit down and map out a new car from scratch – they had to pick up the threads from where John Barnard had left off.

As far as the engine was concerned, we were going to start the season with Porsche, a fact that entailed heavy investment on the part of TAG. But our engineers were working day and night on some new and important modifications which could put us on an equal footing with the redoubtable Honda – the engine we might have had ourselves, all other things being equal . . . .

Another tricky question was who was going to drive alongside me. Rosberg had given us fair warning that he was hanging up his helmet at the end of 1986, and he was as good as his word. There was some talk of Senna, but it was eventually Stefan Johansson who came on board. I didn't know too much about him either, except that Ferrari had let him go, and that Enzo Ferrari had once said in a press conference that Johansson was a fine driver and a fine finisher, but didn't pull his weight in practice.

Before the season started, I took part in all kinds of preliminary trials, sandwiched between a series of promotional appearances for Marlboro in Turkey, Greece, Norway, Sweden and Denmark. Then the 1987 world championship season was on us, starting with the Brazilian Grand Prix.

That race in Brazil will always be one of the most vivid recollections of my Formula One career – for a whole variety of inter-connected reasons.

The McLaren team had been revamped, we had a new car (the MP 4/3) and there were various new boys who had to find their feet and slot into our plans – Murray, Oatley, Johansson. There was the occasional hiccough and the occasional lapse in the chain of command, and the first practice sessions on Friday morning in Rio seemed to take a little longer than usual. However, after a few hours, everything was as before, and the wheels were turning nicely.

To be frank, I was a little confused myself. A few minutes before official practice, two extraordinary things happened. First of all, I bumped into Marco Piccinini, the executive director of the Scuderia Ferrari, who casually remarked: 'You know, Mr Ferrari is still as keen as ever to have you as one of his drivers. If you want to, you can sign a provisional agreement now to drive for him in 1988.' I couldn't help smiling to myself. Ferrari wasn't letting the grass grow under his feet: here we were, practising for the opening Grand Prix of 1987, and he was already making overtures for 1988. On the

Getting ready for Brazil . . .

other hand, this kind of offer is always very flattering and I was
very pleased to be asked.

I should mention that Enzo Ferrari had been after me for some
time to drive one of his cars. I was no sooner back from driving my
very first two Formula One races in 1980 – in Brazil and Argentina
– when the telephone rang at home in Saint Chamond. Anne-Marie
picked it up. It was Marco Piccinini, offering me a cockpit over at
Ferrari.

The second extraordinary thing that happened just before the
1987 Brazilian Grand Prix was that Honda's racing director came
over to me and let it be known that Honda were desperate to have
me as a driver the following season: they would fall in with my
requirements and even build a team around me, anything I wanted.

It was too much for one day. I had to make a determined effort
to put these two conversations behind me if I were to drive at all
decently. Fortunately, there were a number of bugs to be ironed out
of the new McLaren, sufficient to take my mind off these two
fabulous offers. I soon realised that my new car lived up to its
pedigree; with a little work, it would make the grade.

As the representative of the Grand Prix Drivers' Association, I was directly involved in the super licence negotiations in 1987 in Brazil. This photograph of myself and FOCA chief Bernie Ecclestone was taken at the final meeting after the negotiations were concluded

This tiny TV set shows each driver's lap times during practice

That said, we had to face facts on Saturday evening after practice. We were making next to no headway. All we had contrived to do was familiarise ourselves with the car and make a few minor but important adjustments to the cockpit. I dined alone in my room and went to bed early.

On Sunday morning I went out to the circuit very early because I had a major decision to take. Electronic measurement had established that I had excellent top speed at the end of the straight, but I somehow couldn't match the lap times of the Williams or the Lotus. Gordon Murray was in favour of trying to develop better road holding by varying our wing positions. We tried this but it didn't work. Not only did my top speed suffer, I also found that the car handled less well in the corners – it bucked and kicked violently.

I had been around the McLaren for a relatively long time, long enough to know that it holds the road well in its basic configuration and doesn't take kindly to exaggerated wing positions. Accordingly, that Sunday morning, I decided to go back to basics and reduce the front and rear wing settings. That was a tough decision, because Gordon didn't approve and I didn't want to create difficulties in a team that was still in the embryonic stage.

Nevertheless, during warm-up, I discovered that I was right. Half an hour later, I was driving a car that was stable, efficient and powerful. It only dawned on me during the subsequent debriefing that I had made a favourable impression on the squad. Ron Dennis was laughing – which is a fairly rare event – and Johansson kept nodding his head approvingly. I had yet another reason to be pleased.

I made one tiny last-minute adjustment to the suspension which also proved to be right, as I noticed when I made my way to the start.

I was in the third row of the grid, with Senna and Mansell diagonally ahead of me. Mansell got off to a poor start, whereas Piquet, Senna, Fabi and Boutsen shot off into the lead. I was careful not to lose touch with them, but I stuck to my race plan, which was to maintain a steady pace and hold back a little. I knew that tyres were going to be decisive and it was important not to put too much stress on them.

I maintained my rhythm and gradually closed on the lead group, where the Hondas were battling it out, with the lead changing constantly between Piquet, Mansell and Senna. I knew now that I was good enough to mix it with the leaders but, for the time being, the main priority was to keep going. It was at least 40° in the shade that day and the cockpit was like an oven.

I cruised past Mansell and Senna and took over the lead when Piquet went in to change tyres. I chose that moment to indulge in a new luxury: I radioed in to the pits. This was the first time the McLaren had been fitted out with a radio system – and, wonders will never cease, it worked.

The rest of the race was fairly straightforward on the whole, although there were one or two minor incidents.

After the victory celebrations, I set off back to the hotel. It was dusk and, against my better judgement, I was wearing dark glasses. Despite this, I was repeatedly recognised by spectators on their way home and I signed autographs all the way back into Rio. I did so with good grace, because I was in a splendid mood – I had had my little moment of glory.

Winning the first Grand Prix of the season opened up some interesting perspectives. I now knew that I was driving a good car and that, despite formidable opposition from the Williams-Honda, I could be in the running for another world championship title. In fact, I'd been in with a chance every year since 1982, and there weren't many drivers who could make that claim.

I also had another target – the record of outright wins in Formula One. Jackie Stewart had held that distinction since 1973. He had driven to twenty-seven wins, two more than Jim Clark and Niki Lauda. At the end of the 1986 season, I had notched up my twenty-fifth career victory in the Adelaide Grand Prix, to draw level with Clark and Lauda. This latest win in Brazil took me past them into second position behind Jackie Stewart.

There are all sorts of reasons why I didn't win a third title in 1987. For the most part these were technical, often so trivial as to be ridiculous. In the San Marino Grand Prix at Imola, an alternator belt snapped and the engine cut out on me just as I was moving into the lead. Exactly the same thing happened in Germany, after I had shaken off Mansell, Piquet and Senna. And a blown engine in both England and Monaco put paid to my hopes. In Austria, I ground to a halt with a dead battery.

I failed to finish in a long list of races that year. Even when I did finish, all sorts of minor problems pushed me down the points: the Hungarian and French Grand Prix are only two instances out of several.

To my mind, the reason for these innumerable problems was an

Above: *Stefan Johansson joined the McLaren team for the 1987 season, here at Hockenheim*

Right: *Monaco, 1987 – a blown engine ended my hopes*

obvious one. In spite of all the time and money invested, our contract with Porsche had run its term, and the earlier motivation simply wasn't there. In addition, talented as they were, our engineers didn't have the raw material to compete against the industrial might of Honda, whose engine simply steamrollered the opposition.

Nonetheless, amidst this sea of troubles, I did manage to drive to a twenty-seventh Grand Prix victory, equalling Stewart's record.

The venue was Belgium, the circuit Spa-Francorchamps, one of my favourites. My car was in excellent condition on the day, and nothing seemed to go right for my main rivals. Piquet and Alboreto got all tangled together, as did Senna and Mansell, with Ayrton and Nigel later squaring off in the pits and Nigel waving a fist under

Ayrton's nose. While all this was going on, I was driving serenely in the lead, my only problem being that my onboard computer had packed in and I didn't know where I stood in terms of fuel.

Ron Dennis and Steve Nichols did their best to keep me posted via radio, but all I could hear were unintelligible grunts interspersed with bursts of static. When I got down to the last few laps, the only option I could think of was to snatch a quick look at both of them each time I flashed by close to the rail in front of the pits. As long as they remain perfectly calm, I told myself, there surely can't be anything to worry about.

I had my twenty-seven Grand Prix victories, but there was no immediate prospect of a twenty-eighth. Inevitably, I suppose, everyone started asking when the next win would be, to the point where it began to get on my nerves. The season was dragging on and on and I simply wasn't scoring points. In France, the engine was badly tuned; I made a show of challenging Mansell and Piquet but I knew deep down that there was no hope. I was in second place behind Mansell, who had taken the lead after Piquet spun out. Nelson changed tyres and came back into my slipstream. I let him through, because he was genuinely in a position to challenge for the lead, whereas I knew I was out of contention.

I also have less than fond memories of that year's Austrian Grand Prix. Not so much because there were two pile-ups and two restarts, but rather because it is the first and, until now at least, only time in my career with McLaren that I have ever had to bang my fist on the table (in my case, on the steering wheel). I was extremely angry, but my outburst went largely unnoticed, because I was still in my helmet and strapped into the cockpit. Unnoticed, that is, except by Ron Dennis and the McLaren engineers and technicians who had their headphones on.

On Saturday evening I had specified exactly how I wanted the car set up for the Sunday morning warm-up. This being so, I felt quite confident as I drove out onto the circuit. On my very first lap – and on to the fastest stretch of the Österreichring, the straight coming up the Bosch curve – the car got away from me and slewed round broadside at a hundred and ninety miles per hour. By some miracle or other, I got the McLaren back under control fractionally before it ploughed into the crash barriers. It righted itself and I drove slowly back to the pits.

I knew for a fact that I had narrowly missed being killed. After my outburst in the pits, the silence was deafening.

I had matched Jackie Stewart's record of twenty-seven Grand Prix victories, but the twenty-eighth was a long time coming. This is the Austrian Grand Prix, where my battery went dead before the second re-start

All manner of things went wrong during the actual race and, by scraping home only in sixth place in Austria, I lost any real chance of being in the hunt for the world championship. McLaren saw the writing on the wall and immediately set about preparing for the next season. It was at this juncture that Senna's engagement as my teammate in 1988 was officially announced, together with a statement that McLaren would be linking up with Honda in the following year.

The press conference called to announce these changes was held a few days later, in Monza, during the Italian Grand Prix. One fact emerged which caught motor sport *aficionados* by surprise, namely the end of the association between Williams and Honda, all the more remarkable since the 1987 world championship title now seemed certain to go to a Williams driver. Honda, however, was positioning its pieces on a different chessboard: they were only interested in four drivers – Piquet, Senna, Nakajima and myself – and Williams hadn't got the message. Piquet was scheduled to team up with Nakajima the following year at Lotus, and Senna was bound for McLaren. So Williams were minus an engine.

After the Italian Grand Prix, the twelfth race of that season was in Portugal. And it was in Estoril that I finally attained one of my main goals of the 1987 season by driving to my twenty-eighth Formula One victory, taking over the lead from Jackie Stewart in that unofficial but nonetheless highly-regarded all-time Formula One league table.

Estoril was as long and difficult a race as Spa-Francorchamps had been easy. In the first place, I had made something of a hash of qualifying. Then the race had to be restarted, because there was a pile-up very early on. What is more, my first set of tyres – for some unknown reason – was vibrating abominably.

The chase was on as of the thirty-first lap and, believe me, it was quite a chase. Berger was some fifteen seconds up on me, but I was convinced he would be easy meat. I couldn't have been more wrong. I piled on everything I could, driving one fastest lap after another, sliding, opposite-locking, and turning up to full boost (after all, what did I have to lose?). Quite frankly, I don't believe I have ever driven a Formula One race like it.

Berger held on.

Berger wasn't holding me off physically. I wasn't in his slipstream or anything like that. In fact, all he could see was his pit board. My brakes were beginning to overheat and, above all, the McLaren's tyres were taking a terrible beating. I told myself that the same things must be happening to Berger's Ferrari.

I had just corrected the beginnings of a slide when I looked up to see that I was only three seconds behind him. At that moment, there was a little puff of dust up ahead: Berger had spun off. He managed to get the Ferrari back onto the circuit and he came in behind me in second place.

He had lost. I had just won my twenty-eighth Grand Prix.

Jacques Laffite was there. We always stay at the same place in Portugal, in pretty little villas next to a golf course, and he hadn't wanted to miss an opportunity for a game with his friends. Jacques was on top form. The night before he had been even more keyed-up than I was: 'If you win your twenty-eighth tomorrow, we'll paint the town red. On second thoughts, we'll demolish a restaurant!'

We did neither. We spent a quiet, relaxing evening which I enjoyed enormously, as I did the few days that followed, leading up to the Spanish Grand Prix.

In Mexico, with only the Japanese and Australian Grands Prix to come, I finally ruled myself out of the championship race by

Grand Prix win number twenty-eight – at last. I won the Portuguese Grand Prix just as the 1987 season was coming to a close. I don't believe I have ever driven such an aggressive race as I did that day. Victory meant I had beaten Jackie Stewart's record

Trailing Mansell in 1987: the Williams-Honda was unbeatable

clipping Piquet on the first lap. We had mounted different tyre compounds and Nelson had decided to set off slowly. I hit him as I was overtaking. My fault, of course, but he had taken me by surprise by driving so slowly. I retired from the race immediately and Piquet restarted with the aid of a push. There was talk of disqualifying him, and the officials called me in as a witness. I talked them out of it, arguing that Nelson's result should be allowed to stand – it was his race, the championship was obviously going to be between him and Mansell, and we should let them get on with it.

After Mexico, I flew to Japan to take part in the first official nuts-and-bolts meetings between McLaren and Honda, particularly the

Left: With
Nigel Mansell
at Imola

Below:
France 1987: a
badly tuned
engine meant
I was out of
contention

Above left: France 1987: I finished the race but a disappointing third

Top: Belgium 1988: second again to Senna

Above and overleaf: Jacarepagua – a good circuit for me. I notched my fifth win in 1988

Left: Adelaide – always well attended, one of my favourite circuits

Above: My win in the 1988 Grand Prix at Paul Ricard was very satisfying

Below: The Australian Grand Prix of 1988 was a hectic affair, and for me it signalled the victorious end of the turbo era

Above: France 1989: victory, but with Mansell close behind

Below: France 1989 again, with my rival Senna on the inside

Above left: In my new Ferrari during Tests at Estoril just before the start of the 1990 season

Above right and below: A fantastic day for Ferrari and me: a win in Brazil in the second race of the 1990 season

latter's R and D department which supervises Formula One operations on behalf of the Japanese manufacturer.

Quite frankly, I was dazzled. The workshops were so beautifully clean and clinical, genuine laboratories. When I saw the test benches I knew why we had been on a hiding to nothing. The Honda V6 turbo was developing more than 13,600 rpm. When you put this together with the engine's robust construction, it suddenly became clear why Mansell and Piquet had been in their element. I was also shown the Honda 3·5-litre V10 normally-aspirated engine which was to be used by McLaren in the 1989 championship season. The Japanese engineers pointed out modestly that this was only a first attempt . . . .

We had to don white smocks to enter this temple of modern technology. Inside, there were a thousand or so people similarly attired, standing in neat lines waiting to meet us. 'These are your engineers.' My jaw dropped. This was beyond anything I had ever imagined, and I have to say that the world's other automobile engine manufacturers will have to look to their laurels.

According to Ron Dennis, our arrival at the Honda R and D centre started all the girls giggling. My theory is that they had never seen anyone as big as Gordon Murray. But Gordon has his own theory: according to him, it was because they had never seen a nose like mine. It seems that the Asiatics call us Westerners 'long noses'. I keep insisting to Gordon that my nose isn't long, it is simply a bit on the broken side. (I suppose I should have mentioned earlier that I first broke it when I fell off a friend's shoulders while we were horsing around one day. And I broke it again when I went roller-skating. And I broke it again – oh, never mind. . . .)

Our meetings at Honda were over a three-day period and the individual sessions would last for five or more hours at a time. By the end of it all, I came away impressed by three facts about our future partners: their efficiency and pragmatism *vis-à-vis* motor sport, their distaste for preconceived notions about people and concepts, and their appetite for challenge.

Make no mistake about it, they relish a challenge. How else can you account for the fact that they were continuing to develop a turbo engine in 1988 – notwithstanding draconian new regulations introduced by FISA limiting supercharger pressures to 2·5 bar and cutting admissible fuel levels to 150 litres – *and* already working on a brand new normally-aspirated engine.

Ron Dennis and Honda's chief engineer Mr Kawamoto decided

Ayrton Senna congratulated after winning the 1988 Japanese Grand Prix by Emanuele Pirro, who has driven many test miles in the McLaren Honda at Suzuka

that a McLaren should be permanently on hand at the Suzuka circuit as of early 1988 so that testing could be carried out on an ongoing basis. Johansson's name was originally discussed in this connection, but he was taken on by Ligier for the 1988 championship season, and our new man out there is the Italian driver Emanuele Pirro.

18 *Senna's arrival*

As in 1985 and 1986, I was anxious to have a break between championship seasons, not least because the 1988 calendar promised to be a very crowded one. I needed some time to be with my family and friends, to do my own thing. However, despite vehement protestations from Anne-Marie, I also had to spend time on initial tests on the new McLaren-Honda.

One way or another, I managed to fit everything in – including skiing at Meribel and a lot of golf. I have become increasingly addicted to golf in recent years, to the point where Jacques Laffite, Yves Morizot and myself are now the proud owners of a very fine course near Dijon. We acquired it in 1985 and it is going extremely well.

I have always been something of a perfectionist. I am extremely punctilious in everything I am involved in, not only Formula One. As a result, I spend an inordinately long time making doubly certain that any product I endorse is top quality. This holds true for 'Alain Prost' sunglasses manufactured by Pouilloux, for example, or 'Alain Prost' shoes made by Christian Pellet.

I spent a number of long, hard days in Paris filming some publicity spots for Midas. When it was all in the can, the crew clubbed together to buy me an encyclopedia of the cinema; under 'P', they had inserted an additional paragraph which read '*PROST, Alain*, professional actor, hardworking, well-meaning.' I should add that they had really put me through the mill.

One way or another, of course, everything I do is somehow connected with Formula One. This even holds true for the deal I struck with a Swiss firm, Aero-Leasing, to furnish me with a private plane. Some of the other drivers – Piquet, Senna and Berger, to name only three – have had their personal jets for ages, but I always thought it an unnecessary expense. Unnecessary, that is, until I got involved in the Honda programme and the comprehensive series of tests it involves. I finally had to give in to avoid interminable queuing at airport desks.

Despite all this running around, I still managed to find time to relax. I played a lot of golf. When people bring up the question of fatalities in motor racing – and it is a question which crops up time and again in the minds of those who don't really understand the sport or the competitive urge it satisfies – I never hesitate to point out that there are upwards of thirty golfers killed playing the game every year, most of them hit by a wayward tee-shot. There's no getting away from it: golf is a killer sport.

My friend François Illouz, the French amateur golf champion, brought this remarkable statistic to my attention one day when we were playing 18 holes at Spa in Belgium with another friend of mine, Gilles Levent. Gilles hit a full-bodied shot way off target. I managed to duck in the nick of time, but the ball caught François smack on the forehead. As luck would have it, he was wearing a cap. He turned up at the Belgian Grand Prix the following day sporting a magnificent black-and-blue lump . . .

Before the 1988 championship season got underway, there were four major preliminary practice rounds involving most of the top teams. These were held in Estoril, Jerez, Rio and Imola. I handled the first two, and Ayrton Senna took over as of Rio. I decided to go to Brazil as well, however, because I wanted to get a first-hand impression of Senna's debut with McLaren. I am convinced that, had I stayed in Europe, I would have been on tenterhooks waiting for news of how he had coped. You must realise that, even for me, Senna was a big name, bigger even than Rosberg had been one season previously.

Our initial contacts were circumspect. Did Senna have the feeling – totally unwarranted, by the way, although it was often suggested – that he was on Prost territory? Perhaps, perhaps not. But he did act rather like a pampered child – which, I suppose, was perfectly understandable in the circumstances, because up until then his natural ability had always made him the focal point and centre of attraction in any team he had driven for.

To drive home the point that McLaren was a *team*, I stage-managed a little scene for his benefit.

We were in Rio, and I was scheduled to take the wheel to check a few details in the McLaren, after which a new set of tyres would be mounted and Ayrton would take over. There are always little games being played out during unofficial practice: the adrenalin

Trying out the new McLaren-Honda under the watchful eye of designer Steve Nichols and team-mate Ayrton Senna

starts to flow and there is a keen sense of rivalry between the various teams and even between drivers from the same stable, all of them anxious to post the best time. I finished my test laps and came back into the pits. The pit crew started to put on new tyres. And I sat impassively behind the wheel. Ayrton didn't like it. 'It's not fair, it's not fair,' he kept muttering, pacing up and down in the pits. I waited until the new tyres were on and the jacks were removed, then I slowly unbuckled my racing harness.

In the opening stages of the season, Ayrton exhibited another quality: he was meticulous to a fault. He would latch on to every conceivable detail and discuss it *ad nauseam*. I was accustomed to debriefings which lasted perhaps thirty minutes or so. With Senna, you could count on three to four hours. That was simply his way of getting ready for a race. In time, however, and with a bit of compromise on both sides, we developed a good and relaxed working relationship.

He had settled in.

Above: *A word with the great Fangio on the night I was presented with the Champion of Champions Trophy by the Grand Prix Former Drivers Club. McLaren sports director Jo Ramirez is on the left*

Right: *My fifth victory in the Brazilian Grand Prix*

I had some magnificent moments in 1988 both on the track (particularly my victories in the Mexican and French Grands Prix) and away from it. One of the personal highlights was at Monaco, where the former Grand Prix drivers club awarded me their Champion of Champions trophy. (Appropriately enough, I won the Monaco Grand Prix, my twenty-ninth career win.)

At Imola, Arnoux and I were involved in a shunt during qualifying. René has a habit of coming very wide into a corner, so wide that you sometimes get the impression that he is letting you through when, in fact, he is simply cornering after his own fashion. That's what happened at Imola. Afterwards, he came up to me and apologised. He was sincere about it, and that's what counts.

In Hungary, I was obliged to attend an evening reception that wasn't particularly well organised. There was an enormous crush of people there, and they were all over me, calling out, pulling at my clothes, pushing and shoving. I couldn't stand it, so I turned tail and went back up to my hotel room. Ron Dennis looked in on the

The powers-that-be at McLaren: Ron Dennis and Mansour Ojjeh

off chance and spent some time cheering me up. The next day, after some problems during qualifying, I was back in seventh place on the grid. The whole McLaren squad was up at the front, milling round Senna, who had secured the pole position. Right up until the moment the starter flashed the one-minute signal, Ron Dennis stood at the safety barrier right beside me. It was a simple gesture of friendship, but it was nonetheless touching.

Senna got the upper hand as the season progressed.

For one thing, he was better during qualifying because he was more familiar with the Honda engine, having driven with it in the previous season. Also, in the corners, he has developed a technique of applying successive touches to the accelerator which exploits the Honda's power to the full and allows our technicians to get the most out of the engine by boosting the turbo pick-up interval. I have tried occasionally during qualifying to imitate Ayrton's staccato driving style, but I have never succeeded.

During an actual race, Senna played two trump cards: he used my settings, because he knows – and has always been the first to admit – that I am better at setting-up than he is, and he takes the

Imola 1988

Trailed by Philippe Alliot in the Lola at Montreal

kind of major risk which I choose not to take. This said, I believe that, with a naturally-aspirated engine, he will no longer be able to drive in the same fashion in 1989.

There is nothing mysterious or magical about Formula One – everything is logical and everything has an explanation. If I no longer believed in myself, or if I admitted to myself that Senna were the better driver, I would have no hesitation in looking elsewhere for a cockpit in 1989. This is not the case: Senna and I will be together in the McLaren next season.

I tried to explain as much to a small group of journalists – who were obviously incapable of appreciating what driving is all about

138

– after I had failed to finish in the British Grand Prix. It was raining, which was clearly not particularly to my liking, but I have driven some excellent races in the wet. But I had a problem and it was a major one: during the previous Grand Prix, in France, I had driven over a kerb and damaged the superstructure of the McLaren. We hadn't realised it at the time, but I found out with a vengeance during the British Grand Prix: the superstructure had lost all rigidity and was causing me to understeer and oversteer in every corner. In the rain, it was catastrophic. I was driving half blind, way down the field, and there was nothing in it for me – except, perhaps, a serious accident. I chose to retire.

A few days later, I started to see all manner of inane comments in the press. Prost had lost his nerve. Prost had chickened out. Prost was exhausted after winning the French Grand Prix. And so on. That was how the sensationalist press elected to report the incident. I expressed my displeasure in no uncertain terms.

Still, you have to learn to separate the wheat from the chaff. I count among my closest friends three or four journalists that I trust implicitly and who know all there is to know about me. I talk to them frankly and honestly and, in return, they are in a position to report facts rather than fiction.

I have always believed in telling the truth.

19 *Putting my foot down*

After the British Grand Prix, where I had deliberately chosen not to finish, I came second in each of the next three races. The first of these was the German Grand Prix, where I learned a thing or two.

I damaged the McLaren's superstructure during qualifying when I swerved to miss a Eurobrun and climbed all over the kerb. As a result, the reserve car was readied for the race itself. I had already noticed during qualifying that Honda had put an old engine into my McLaren and, during the actual race, I seem to remember a whole batch of niggling little problems connected with the engine and with the way the car had been set up.

For all that, I was quite content with my second place result, if only for the simple reason that the race had been in the wet and I had made a pretty good job of handling the conditions. In fact, I had gone into a spin in the very first corner, corrected it and worked my way back up through the field extremely well – shaking off Nannini and then Berger before setting off in pursuit of Senna. The circuit was like an ice rink and I was driving a car set up for dry conditions. I nudged both Nakajima and Arnoux as I was lapping them, and a spin forced me to settle for second place. At any event, I had given the lie to those who said I wasn't up to scratch in the wet. With a good car, I had no doubt that I could hold my own.

My second place in the Hungarian Grand Prix left a bitter taste in my mouth. I had everything going for me and I was the quickest on the day, as my fastest lap shows.

Two factors combined to push me back into second place. First, there was the fact that I started back in seventh place on the grid; I hadn't been able to improve on this because I simply didn't get a clear round during the final qualifying session on the tortuous Budapest circuit. Second, just as I was finally overtaking Senna (after having made one attempt a few laps previously), the front left

140

wheel started to shudder in alarming fashion. I was obliged to ease up for a while. Then, once I had established that the problem was not getting any worse, I put on the pressure again and went back on the attack. It was too late – I crossed the line half a second behind Senna.

My second place in the Belgian Grand Prix, once again behind Ayrton, can be ascribed to problems of an entirely different nature. I had set the car up in a most satisfactory way but, as Ayrton had duplicated my settings, I decided to modify them slightly at the very last moment, while we were on the starting grid. I took off some wing to boost my top speed and cut back on my fuel consumption. This was a risky move, but it could well have turned out favourably.

As it happened, my last-minute decision proved to be a mistake. It took next to no time to establish that the car was misbehaving; what is more, the surface had broken up and my tyres were

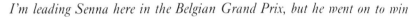

I'm leading Senna here in the Belgian Grand Prix, but he went on to win

suffering. There was no way I could match Senna's pace and rhythm.

By this juncture, Ayrton had seven wins to his credit and I was lagging behind on four. McLaren had won the first eleven races of the championship season and, as things stood, it was very much on the cards that we would win every single Grand Prix. If that happened, the title would be decided on the number of outright wins and place points wouldn't enter into the reckoning. I said as much at the press conference immediately following the Belgian Grand Prix, adding that Senna had already done enough to deserve the title and that he would make a worthy world champion.

After the traditional interviews were over, I went back for another look at my McLaren. Neil Oatley was standing beside it. I was puzzled by the effect of the virtually imperceptible adjustments I had made at the eleventh hour, albeit by guesswork, and I simply couldn't fathom why the car had reacted so badly. It didn't take Neil long to establish why the underbody had scraped the circuit throughout the entire race and why the car had handled so poorly. The tyre pressures were totally out of synch, front and back. If anything, poor Neil was even more crestfallen than I was. I tried to wipe the scowl off his face by remarking philosophically: 'That's life, Neil, there'll be other races.'

The Italian Grand Prix was next on the agenda. Both McLarens failed to finish. Senna was involved in a shunt with Schlesser. As for myself, I fell victim to a most unusual problem which nonetheless seemed to be par for the course that season: my engine blew. Obviously, these things happen: a blown engine is not all that out of the ordinary *per se*, but this was the very first time it had happened to one of our McLarens – and it had to happen to mine.

You will appreciate that I was absolutely furious. Although I could feel the Honda's power ebbing away, I decided not to stop, despite frantic signals to that effect from the pits: I wanted the damn thing to explode. I pushed it for all it was worth for six whole laps, then I reappraised the situation. Perhaps the problem was a minor one that the mechanics could try to remedy; perhaps I could get back into the race and possibly drive at least the fastest lap (and satisfy my obsession with records). I finally pulled off into the pits, but the diagnosis proved fatal: broken piston.

Senna hadn't been able to finish either, so we were back where we started on the day. All the same, I couldn't help giving vent to my frustration: to me, it seemed absolutely inconceivable that I could be the victim of such a long chapter of misfortune, dating back to the French Grand Prix, involving either the McLaren chassis or the Honda engine. I am convinced that the McLaren-Honda team took my point and made a very special effort to remedy the situation as of the next Grand Prix in Portugal.

When I arrived in Estoril, I was in peak condition both physically and mentally. I had invited my parents to come down with me, and we had rented houses – together with my friends Johnny, Gilles and Jean-Louis – at our usual spot at Quinta de Marinha, a few kilometres from the Estoril circuit. Piquet, Berger, Alliot and Dalmas were also there, as were some of my childhood friends from Saint Chamond, who had chartered a plane to come and support me. Believe me, dinners out were very boisterous affairs . . . .

After Monza, I had treated myself to a few days of total rest back home in Switzerland, dividing my time between my family and the golf course. I also kept one eye on the 1988 Olympics and the other on Senna's progress as he tested the 3·5-litre naturally-aspirated Honda. It appeared that he and the McLaren 'atmos' weren't exactly seeing eye to eye: he had already been in a shunt at Silverstone with the new car, and he bent the chassis again when he made another unscheduled exit.

When we got to the Estoril circuit on the Friday morning, I was raring to go. There was a spanking new chassis waiting for me, together with engines that I considered nothing short of perfect. I made pole position after a stirring duel with Ayrton.

Just before the start of the race, I took a couple of extra precautions: I marginally changed the car's aerodynamics and modified the tyre pressure. And I asked Jo Ramirez to brush the dust away from the track diagonally ahead of my front wheels. Pole position is on the right of the grid at Estoril, where there is very little traffic, since all the cars swing out left to take the double right-hander which comes immediately after the start. The last thing I wanted was to flounder about in a dust cloud when the green light came on.

There were three 'starts' to that Grand Prix – the first countdown was interrupted, and the second one saw us get away only to be flagged down after one lap because of a multiple shunt. During the second start, I noticed that Senna got away from the grid much better than I did: I had been obliged to stay in the middle of the circuit to find some semblance of a line into the right-hander, but he had gone through it with no problem whatsoever.

The third start was good. I went off as before. As I was lining the car up, I squeezed Ayrton ever so slightly over towards the offside white line. I was level with him and just about to brake for the double right-hander when he swooped across to the inside as if I didn't exist. I slammed on the brakes and just missed hitting him.

I knew from the very first lap that my car was significantly outperforming his. As we were coming past the pits just before the start of lap two, I pulled out to overtake. God only knows what possessed him at that moment. Whatever it was, he swung over towards the wall on the right, squeezing me between his car and the wall so tightly that our wheels dovetailed. To my right, I had only millimetres to spare – as a couple of pit crews will testify, since they had to hurl themselves backwards to avoid my helmet smashing through their signal boards. And I couldn't afford to hit the brakes: if I did, the cars behind would have no chance of avoiding an accident. What is more, if I braked, our wheels would interlock and he would shoot straight up into the air, possibly into the pits or into the crowd. I had no option. I snapped the steering wheel over to the left and back – very quickly – and that forced him to break away. I was through.

I drove an excellent race and Capelli turned out to be a fine competitor. Nevertheless, even on the podium and during the press conference, I had to force myself to smile. Ayrton's manoeuvre really stuck in my gorge.

I caught up with him a few hours later, sitting in the McLaren trailer with Osamu Goto. And I told him what I thought of him. I asked him point blank if he had gone off his head. He retorted that I had squeezed him at the start of the race. I wasn't having any of that: 'What I did at the start was completely above board. I left room for you. I couldn't see you in my rear mirror, so I didn't move over. I did exactly the same thing at the second start, and the plain fact is that you went through ahead of me both times. Anyway, that has nothing to do with what you did at the end of the first lap: that was inexcusable.'

Ayrton apologised. You could have cut the atmosphere with a knife, but I believe he didn't want to do any permanent damage to our relationship.

In Spain, one week after Estoril, I won my thirty-fourth Grand Prix. Between the two races, I had popped over to Paris to visit the *Salon de l'Automobile* and to take part in a press conference organised by Honda. An incredibly silly episode ensued.

A sensation-hungry journalist decided to eavesdrop on a private conversation I was having with Stefan Johansson. I say 'eavesdrop' because he wasn't invited to join the conversation and he couldn't have heard more than an occasional snippet. What he cobbled together was, needless to say, a complete distortion; Stefan, thank God, can bear witness to that. I mentioned to Stefan at one point that there seemed to be marginal differences in our Honda engines. Note the word 'seemed'. This second-rate hack contrived to fabricate a piece which had Prost alleging that his engine was at times at a forty to fifty horsepower disadvantage by comparison with Senna's. Absolute rubbish! Nevertheless, I had to take time in Paris to clear the air with Honda. The self-same hack turned up in the McLaren trailer a few days later, in Spain. I had the pleasure of turfing him out: he deserved it.

The Spanish Grand Prix was a difficult race. I didn't make pole position but I was well-positioned on the open side. When the green

Jerez 1988 – a difficult race, with Nigel Mansell in the Williams as tenacious as ever

light came on, I went off in the lead without too much trouble, with Mansell snapping at my heels. Senna was out of the running – definitively, as it turned out – but Mansell in the Williams proved to be just as tenacious an opponent on the track as he is on the golf course, where he excels. I had the devil of a job trying to shake him off. Worse, I soon realised that I wouldn't be able to stick to my pre-race plan of making it through to the finish on the same set of tyres. Worse still, my radio was on the blink and I couldn't alert the pit crew.

Fortunately, eagle-eyed Ron Dennis cottoned on to what was happening: he waited until I had pulled sufficiently far ahead of Mansell, then signalled me in by the simple expedient of sticking an arrow on the pit board. I changed tyres – nearly stalling in the process – and everything went much, much better from then on. I was able to take charge of the race right through to the flag. I had notched up another Grand Prix; more important, that victory in Spain put me back in with a chance in the title hunt.

After Spain, my clash with Senna during the Portuguese Grand Prix was again news. We had come within a hair's breadth of catastrophe on the circuit and we had also come very, very close to breaking point in our relationship (which would have certainly poisoned the atmosphere within the squad and ended up with who knows what dire consequences for one or the other of us). Once he was back home in Brazil, however, Senna suddenly wasn't all that certain any more that I had been in the right. He said so in an interview and I replied in a follow-up interview that he was just a spoilt brat.

He had his way of building tension in the run-up to the Japanese Grand Prix – and I had mine. In Suzuka, of course, the championship could be decided once and for all. Ayrton only had to score one more victory to wrap up the title; as for me, I had to come in anywhere, provided it was ahead of him, both in Suzuka and in Adelaide, to pip him at the post. In other words, I had to outperform him in Suzuka to keep the title race open until Adelaide.

On the Friday morning in Suzuka, I was not in the best of shape. I had spent a sleepless night because of jet lag, and my insides were playing me up. In spite of this, all went fairly well that morning, and I was easily fastest in practice. The chassis and engine seemed to be just right.

My world was stood on its head during the first qualifying session. The engine started acting up and the chassis lost all its earlier efficiency. I somehow contrived to drive the third best time – behind Senna and Berger – although I had spent most of the session in fourth place, behind those two and Mansell.

My first inclination was to put the blame on the engine. It appeared that it was powerful enough to develop a good top speed, but strangely rough at lower revs, which detracted from the performance of the chassis and precluded any improved settings. In fact, the problem was of a different order entirely. Tim Wright, who had stepped in as my race engineer in Neil Oatley's absence (Neil was tied up in Woking at the time, working on the design of the 1989 McLaren), put his finger on the problem. We now had new front ailerons complete with skirts whose height could be adjusted via a system of grooves. These had first seen the light of day in Portugal, but we hadn't had time to try them out; as a result, it was in Japan that they were fitted on my car for the first time. It emerged that the skirts themselves promptly went out of balance; worse, the material they were made of was too soft and it, too, quickly deteriorated. The upshot was that the McLaren's overall aerodynamics were totally disrupted.

Once we had identified the problem, I was convinced that I would be able to improve matters on the Saturday. I was wrong. I was working with the reserve car (which was actually Senna's race car, because Ayrton had opted to work with the original reserve car to check his settings) and I decided to split my practice session into two parts, first working on the reserve with a full tank, then with my race car on a virtually empty tank. I did one quick lap in the reserve and came back into the pits as fast as I could. I dashed over to the little prefabricated hut that served as team trailer, furiously stripping off my all-in-one: the tank, full of petrol, had voided and I had been treated to a high-octane hip bath.

Clearly, my practice session was as good as over, because I now had to fill up the race car, then drain it to get ready for qualifying.

Tim Wright and I talked things over between 'practice' and qualifying. There was a lot of setting-up still to do and I hounded everybody remorselessly. By that afternoon, the car was back in shape.

Now it was my turn to behave like a novice. As I was coming up to the end of a very fast lap which, I am certain, would have qualified me in pole position, I missed a gear – a lapse in concentration which I can only ascribe to being too sure of myself. On previous laps I had been coming through this point at about 170 mph. On this, my best lap, I posted an appalling 159 mph.

147

There was no point in dwelling on it, however, and I now knew that I had a decent chassis and a decent engine. On the Sunday, I ran my habitual checks on my race car and was perturbed to find that the engine was stuttering at low revs. What is more, the pop-off valve was opening at 2·45 bar. The mechanics changed it, and the McLaren seemed in best order as we drove some warm-up laps and took our places on the grid.

There was unfortunately one other problem on my mind. A slight drizzle began to fall only minutes before the actual start. This convinced me that I should make one or two minor last-minute adjustments to the settings. I took off the front suspension chocks to smooth the ride. If it really rained, so much the better. The green light came on and the race was underway.

Senna won the Japanese Grand Prix and, with it, his first world championship title. He got off to a poor start but he clawed himself back into the race in spectacular fashion.

I had my fair share of problems that day, and that must have made things easier for him. After a few laps, my gearbox started acting up, and I was soon in trouble changing up and down into second and third. If you followed the race on television, you will have noticed that, because of this, I often had difficulty negotiating the corners, particularly the chicane. It was not until a few days later that we finally discovered what had happened: the clutch had worn down progressively.

In addition to my gear-change problem, I had a hard time getting through the backmarkers, some of whom were distinctly reticent about moving over – notably De Cesaris and Gugelmin. Unfortunately, Ayrton is more aggressive and more skilful in this particular respect, and he found it quite easy to reel me in, pass me and drive to victory.

I was intrigued to learn later that, as Senna flashed over the line to victory, the Honda mechanics went wild with delight. As for me, there was a major consolation in that moment of defeat: I sensed very keenly how supportive my family and close friends were, not to mention many of the people on the McLaren side. (In fact, just before the Japanese Grand Prix, there had been a straw poll in Woking to establish who they wanted, deep down, to win the title, and I had come out clearly ahead.)

There was what one might call an 'incident' immediately after the finish of the Japanese Grand Prix. Ron Dennis had left right away to catch a flight back to England: for several weeks now, his

*Ayrton Senna on the way to the victory in Japan which clinched the 1988
World Championship. Ivan Capelli in the March (rear) briefly led the race*

wife had been in poor health and she was going through a particularly bad patch. Senna and I were fielding questions from the press, and both of us were rather angry about the behaviour of the backmarkers, not only in this particular Grand Prix but throughout the season as a whole. We both stressed that FISA might be well advised to take a stand on this issue.

The powers-that-be took a stand all right, but on a completely different matter. As I said, I had had gear-change problems right through the race (at this point, I didn't yet know that the clutch was the root cause). Suddenly, the Federation insisted that its technicians be on hand while the McLaren gearboxes were dismantled, as they had to be before the cars were crated off to Australia. The only information they gleaned from this operation, by the way, was that my box was slightly damaged by comparison with Senna's.

A little later, I was asked by the French media whether I thought that Senna had been treated more favourably than myself. I said what I have always thought – and never tried to hide – namely that McLaren had tended to pay more attention to Senna than to myself, since he was the new boy in the squad and it was essential that he feel accepted and be integrated as quickly as possible. Moreover, he had worked with Honda longer than I had, he was better acquainted with the technicians and, figuratively at least, he was able to talk their language. The Japanese are highly sensitive to bonds of friendship and culture and, as a result, had undoubtedly favoured Ayrton by paying more attention to his problems than to mine.

I arrived in Tokyo the following morning, *en route* for Cairns and Port Douglas in Australia, where I was planning a short vacation. I gave a couple of interviews and, a week later, I was back in Adelaide, ready for the final Grand Prix of the 1988 championship season.

Shell organised a press conference late on the Thursday afternoon. This tends to be a harmless, laid-back affair, designed principally to introduce the drivers to the Australian media. Not so this time. It was a major event, and a good slice of the international press was on hand.

Ron Dennis came straight in from the airport to join Senna and myself, and he wasted no time getting down to brass tacks. First of all, he was highly critical of the letter sent to Honda by the President of the International Federation stipulating that our engine suppliers should henceforth be scrupulously equitable in their preparation of engines for the two drivers in the McLaren team. Honda's reply, despite its formality and circumlocutions, was scathing.

Ron then moved on to the next issue – in his eyes, a much more serious one – namely the Federation's insistence that its technicians be on hand during dismantling of the McLaren gearboxes following the Japanese Grand Prix. In essence, his view was that this constituted a dangerous precedent. Apart from the possible impropriety it implied, there were a number of technical aspects which he would have preferred to remain undisclosed, e.g., the McLaren differential.

He then went on to say that McLaren had always treated its drivers on a strictly equal footing, although this was of course extremely difficult in the case of such high-tech racing machines. This being so, he viewed as negligible all the various problems that I had encountered in the course of the season. In other words, if Ron were to be believed, 1988 had been plain sailing for me.

I am an understanding sort of person, and I am quick to make allowances. I accept most things, but I won't be treated like an imbecile. What about my trials and tribulations in England? In Germany? In Hungary? In Belgium? In Italy? These had simply been glossed over.

I held my temper in check until after the press conference. However, once we got outside, I made my views clear to Ron. I didn't pull any punches. At that moment, I felt no affinity with McLaren. We were in the forecourt of the Shell station that adjoins the Adelaide circuit, hardly the time or place to debate matters. Accordingly, we agreed to get together again at the dinner scheduled that evening in honour of our technicians.

I stuck to my guns over dinner and Ron proposed a further rendezvous at breakfast the following morning: there would be just the two of us and I would drive him out to the circuit afterwards. I made my views clear once again and, little by little, the fog lifted. Ron admitted what I had always suspected: for a good part of the season, the McLaren-Honda pairing had lavished attention on Ayrton in the belief that he needed support to fit into the team.

Once that was out in the open, I was able to face the last Grand Prix of the season with a certain degree of new-found equanimity. But I left Ron Dennis in no doubts on two matters. First, whatever the future holds, I will not be in a hurry to forget what happened; and, second, I insisted on a restructuring of McLaren's way of doing things before the start of the 1989 championship season.

I desperately wanted to end the season with a win in Adelaide

1988 record-breaking Marlboro-McLaren team

The Australian Grand Prix was a hectic affair all round –
practice, qualifying and the race itself. This was to be the last
Grand Prix of the turbo era, which had begun in 1977 at the British
Grand Prix at Silverstone when my friend Jean-Pierre Jabouille first
drove the 1500 cc Renault Formula One Turbo. I had been one of
the pioneers of the age of the turbo and all my triumphs had been
during it. I was desperately anxious to sign off with a flourish. And
I did.

I finished the season in Adelaide with a win, bringing my season's
total to seven first places and seven second places – fourteen results
in sixteen Grands Prix. In my view, that is nothing to be ashamed
of. I have now driven to thirty-five Formula One victories: a record.
I racked up 105 points in the 1988 championship, more than any
other driver has ever achieved in a single season: another record.
Since my first race back in 1980, I have amassed a total of 511·5
Formula One points, ahead of Niki Lauda on 420·5: yet another
record. And I have now equalled Jim Clark's record of twenty-seven
fastest laps in Formula One.

All things considered, not bad going. . . .

20 *Image and fame*

By the end of 1988 I had been in Formula One for nine seasons, nine years of my life and my family's life dictated by the Grand Prix calendar. I have attempted in this book to give a warts-and-all account of a racing driver's life, and I have also tried to explain what it takes to succeed in this profession. In fact, it is a profession just like any other, and making a success of it is a question of taking control of events and coming to terms with one's destiny. Being a racing driver is a complex business, because the normal problems of everyday life are compounded by the risks implicit in the sport. One of my priorities has always been to cut these risks to a minimum.

There is one aspect of racing driving, however, with which I have never quite been able to come to terms: for want of a better word, call it stardom. My life would be complete if it weren't for this eternal constraint that forces me to keep a low profile when I would far rather be just another face in the crowd.

My father comes to the occasional Grand Prix: he keeps smiling and keeps in the background

This is one for Ron Dennis. . .

It is sometimes said that I am conceited. I know this for a fact, because my father occasionally comes along to watch a Grand Prix. No-one knows him. He listens to what is being said around him and he tells me afterwards. It never fails to amuse me. I am not conceited, but the chances are that I have chosen that particular day to pull someone else down a peg or two. There is nothing I can do about it. When I am playing golf and I fluff an easy chip, I am the first to shout at myself: 'You ugly little bastard!'

During unofficial practice this year in Jerez, I was walking through the foyer of the hotel. Josele Garza, the Indycar driver, came by and stuck his hand out in greeting. Apparently I walked straight past without noticing him. In the restaurant a few minutes later, Luis Perez-Sala, the Formula 3000 champion who was going to be driving Formula One for the first time that season, flashed a broad grin in my direction. I didn't react. It was only afterwards that my friends tactfully pointed out who they were. I was terribly embarrassed, but it was too late. I doubt if either Garza or Perez-Sala has a very high opinion of me.

I would love to be able to go to a movie in peace. When I visit the cinema these days, I have to don a beret and put on a false moustache.

Not so very long ago, I was skiing in Meribel. I had found a huge balaclava helmet and I was wearing outsize ski goggles. Just as I was about to launch myself downhill, a perfect stranger standing next to me tapped me on the shoulder: 'Ça va, Alain?'. . . .

155

21 *Champion Again*

Derick Allsop, in interviews with Alain Prost, brings the story up-to-date

DERICK ALLSOP: Alain Prost was entitled to be optimistic about his prospects for the 1989 World Championship. McLaren had a proven package that seemed under no immediate threat. Ferrari, who had employed Nigel Mansell, were hopeful that John Barnard's 640 would emerge as a genuine contender. The seven-speed, semi-automatic gearbox gave the Italian car a potential advantage, but the team had done relatively little testing and couldn't count on its reliability. Williams, in partnership now with Renault, would also need time, while Benetton still appeared to be a safe distance behind. It all pointed to McLaren Honda's year again. And this one might be Alain's. Despite that incident with Senna in Portugal and his wider concerns, he had cleared the air with Ron Dennis and was at peace with the world.

ALAIN PROST: At the start of the season I felt fine. There were pressures in '88 and my relationship with Ayrton was not fantastic, but it was never bad. I had to speak to him after the race at Estoril because that was the best thing to do. After that I hoped it would be finished. Then you have the winter, you come back and everything seems OK again. All you want to think about is the racing, not problems.

DA: Both McLaren drivers had problems in Brazil, but Prost came out of it better than his partner. Senna collided with Gerhard Berger's Ferrari on the first corner and was immediately out of contention for points. Prost was restricted by clutch trouble, didn't dare risk a tyre stop and soldiered on for a sensible second place behind Mansell. Ferrari and the Englishman couldn't believe their luck and it wouldn't last. At Imola, in fact, near tragedy awaited the 'home' team. Berger went straight on at the left sweep into Tamburello. The car smashed into a wall, then burst into flames. Amazingly, the Austrian escaped with minor burns and missed only one further race.

The San Marino Grand Prix was clearly going to be dominated by the McLarens. To avert any risks to each other, Prost and Senna agreed that neither would attempt to overtake the other at the first corner. Good thinking, commendable teamwork. Alain still thought so as he led from the restart – only to see the other McLaren dive past him into the first corner. The order stayed like that for the rest of the race. Alain was furious, as his expression at the end revealed. It was the beginning of the end of their fragile relationship.

AP: It all changed at Imola. We had an agreement and he broke it. What he did was dishonest and dishonourable. I knew then that I could never trust him again. I could have hit him. That would have been one solution. I'm not joking . . .

DA: Before the Monaco Grand Prix, however, Dennis tried to convince the media that his was a 'fun' team and that the little difference between his two drivers had been resolved. Senna had, indeed, made a tearful admission about the pact, though he later defended his manoeuvre on the grounds that he had taken Alain before the braking area. They resumed their duel in the Principality and again victory went to the Brazilian, who managed to cover up a gearbox problem. Prost was held up by Rene Arnoux and then lost half a minute as Nelson Piquet and Andrea De Cesaris sat in the middle of the road at Loews Hairpin, trading abuse and accusations.

AP: I was almost laughing when I came up to their accident. It was a joke. It is ridiculous to have to stop like that in Formula One. But I had to. There was nothing else I could do. As for Arnoux, well that was bad. It was not the first time that had happened. But I have to say my biggest problem was that I was not aggressive enough. Ayrton is much more aggressive than I am in traffic.

DA: Prost's three second places and Senna's two wins left them level at the top of the Championship table, already destined to be a domestic affair. After the Mexican Grand Prix Senna had a seven-point lead. Alain made a rare miscalculation in his tyre selection, an error compounded by the team when he stopped to change rubber. The upshot was fifth place, while his team-mate had a third win. Alain also suspected Senna had a superior engine . . .

The pendulum began to swing the other way in the first Grand Prix held on the streets of Phoenix, Arizona. An electronics fault put Senna out of the contest, leaving Prost to claim his first victory of the season and edge a couple of points ahead in the Championship. Both men were out of luck at a wet Montreal, where Thierry Boutsen and the Williams-Renault had their first success. Before the French Grand Prix Alain made his long awaited announcement: he would be leaving McLaren at the end of the season. But where to? At that stage, he wasn't saying. There was speculation that he might form his own team, or retire, or merely have a sabbatical. Certainly there would be no shortage of offers from other teams. All he would talk about were his reasons for leaving, and in reality that came down to one reason – Senna.

AP: Having finally made the decision to leave McLaren I felt more relaxed. I have to admit that in 1989, for the first time in my career, I lost some motivation. For six years the McLaren team had been like my family, with a wonderful, friendly atmosphere. But in '89 it became awful. Senna didn't speak, didn't smile. The difference between us was that I worked for McLaren, while Senna worked for Senna.

DA: Nothing worked for Senna that weekend. Alain beat him to pole and comfortably won the race. Senna had a transmission failure before the first corner. Another win in the British Grand Prix at Silverstone, after his partner went off, left the Frenchman with a 20-point lead at the top of the table.

Alain lost sixth gear and conceded the race to Senna in Germany, while both McLarens were outclassed by Mansell's Ferrari at the winding Hungaroring. Second place behind Senna at a wet Spa kept Prost 11 points clear as he headed for Monza and a rapturous welcome from the *tifosi*. Alain had decided to drive for Ferrari in 1990, and now it was official.

AP: I thought very carefully about my future. I did seriously consider retiring. It was certainly one of my options. But as the weeks went by that summer I began to think more and more in terms of driving for another team. I spoke to many people but in the end it came down to two possibilities – Williams and Ferrari. The problem with Williams was that they were very late with the new car. How could I sign for them without seeing the car and without knowing exactly what was happening?

I did not want to do one more year just for an extra contract. I wanted a competitive car. As soon as I felt sure the Ferrari would be competitive for 1990 I decided to join them. I thought the car and the team had the potential and by the end of the season I was even more convinced I had made the right decision. Straightaway I was more motivated and began to look forward to the following season. I would have preferred John Barnard to stay with Ferrari instead of going to Benetton, but he had his reasons so that was that.

DA: First, though, he had some unfinished '89 business. His suspicions about favouritism towards Senna deepened over the weekend of the Italian Grand Prix. Senna was 1.79 seconds faster in qualifying and was on course for an easy win until his engine blew. Prost had the victory, his 20-point advantage was restored and he was the hero of Italy. He responded to the fans by offering them his trophy from the podium, much to the dispproval of Dennis. Even the McLaren boss couldn't now pretend their friendship was intact.

AP: Nothing would work on my car in practice, which I found very puzzling. All right, so Senna might have been faster, but not by nearly two seconds. That does not make sense. The fact that his engine blew up in the race didn't change my feelings. Perhaps he had too much power! I was frustrated because I couldn't catch him. I wasn't happy with the engines, but what could I do? I felt I had to talk about it. I had what would have been a good lead in normal circumstances, but I felt that anything could have happened in the four remaining races.

The problem was one of ego. Some people could not stand to lose the No. 1 to another team. The number meant nothing to me, but to some it did. The reception I got at Monza was because I had just signed for Ferrari and I enjoyed it. That's why I reacted the way I did with the trophy. It was not because I was not supposed to do it and someone would not like it. We are sportsmen and we should enjoy occasions such as that. Everybody talks about business and politics, but at the end of the day we are sportsmen. When you arrive on the podium after winning the race in front of 100,000 people and they are applauding you, you don't think about anything else. Nobody else exists. You just take the pleasure because that is part of the sport.

DA: Prost's 39th Grand Prix win was followed by more pleasure in Portugal, even though he was second behind Berger's Ferrari. His title lead stretched to 24 points (under the Championship rules he could count only his best 11 scores) because Senna had collided and spun off with Mansell. The Englishman had been shown the black flag after reversing in the pit-lane and insisted he hadn't seen it. He was later banned from the Spanish Grand Prix and fined 50,000 dollars. Senna said he hadn't seen it either, though there were conflicting reports on his view.

AP: I can swear that in Portugal it was very difficult to see. I cannot believe that a driver, any driver, can see the black flag for two or three laps and still fight another car. At first Ayrton said that he saw the black flag but then changed his mind and said he didn't, so how do you know? In his position I would have let Nigel pass anyway because he could not have stood in his way for the whole of the race. But then Ayrton does not like to be passed by anyone.

DA: Prost was in no position to pass Senna in Spain. He described his car as a 'taxi' and had to settle for third place. He promised he would be more motivated in Japan, where Senna had to win to stay in contention for the crown. Alain went to Suzuka to attack, and opened up with strong words:

AP: Senna is a man who just lives for and thinks about competition. He has abandoned everything else, every human relationship. He feels sustained by God and he is capable of taking every risk because he thinks he is immortal.

DA: The remarkable events of that race day were matched only by the remarkable events of the following weeks and months. Prost, as good and positive as his word, went clear, and although Senna retaliated the title leader stood his ground. Senna, having nothing to lose, dived inside at the chicane and the McLarens had the inevitable coming-together. Prost climbed out, only to watch in astonishment as Senna demanded a push-start, returned to the track from the back of the chicane and went into the pits for repairs. He regained the lead from Alessandro Nannini's Benetton – at the chicane – and took the chequered flag.

Officialdom, though, had seen more than it could take and Senna was disqualified for missing the chicane after his collision with his team-mate. Prost was declared champion for a third time. Rather than celebrate, McLaren protested on Senna's behalf. 'Our duty is to try to win every race,' they explained. Prost's reaction was understandable:

AP: This has been my worst Formula One season, especially on the human side. I knew something like this could happen. Senna can't accept that someone might resist him trying to overtake. The way he drives is quick, but too hard. If you had two drivers like that, you would have accidents in every race.

DA: FIA not only threw out the appeal, but also cited five other indiscretions by Senna, fined him 100,000 dollars and handed him a suspended six-month ban. McLaren declared their intention to fight on – in the civil courts if necessary – but Prost would be recognised as champion no matter what happened in Australia.

What happened in Australia was more drama and controversy. Torrential rain made the track treacherous and Prost led the drivers' resistance against racing. The start was delayed but as the re-appointed time approached the drivers drifted back to their cars. Prost joined them – for one lap. He then pulled into the pits. A lap later the action was stopped. Prost refused to line-up for the re-start and subsequent incidents did nothing to convince him he was wrong. Senna was among those lucky to escape serious injury when he ran into the back of Martin Brundle's Brabham. Now there was no way the Brazilian could keep his title. The race was won by Boutsen.

AP: I couldn't understand the sense in people going out there in conditions like that. You've got only one life. All the work we had done in the years past had gone to waste.

DA: It was an unsatisfactory end to a largely unsatisfactory year. But Alain had his third title. Only one other driver, Juan Manuel Fangio, with five, had won it more often and only four others,

Brabham, Stewart, Lauda and Piquet, had won it as many times. He had also extended his record total of Grand Prix wins to 39. And, spreading out in front of him, was a new challenge. With Ferrari, and with Mansell.

AP: Even if I'd signed another contract with McLaren, even if the relationship had been good, I think I would have regretted staying. After six years I think I had already been there too long. There was no joy, no pleasure, in having to fight someone in an unfair way. I just went there and clocked on like a production-line worker at Renault or Peugeot.

Now I have the motivation again. My biggest motivation is to help Ferrari win the Championship. I would prefer to win it myself, but if Nigel wins it will still be a victory for me. To be part of a team, that's what I like. That's what matters. I am sure there will be no problem working with Nigel. We have been friends for a long time and we were soon working well together. He is very fast, very motivated, but we communicate.

That is the great thing about Ferrari. Everybody talks. I missed that in my last two years at McLaren. And it is only when you join Ferrari that you find out just how fantastic it is. You are driving not only for a team but a whole country. All Italy wants you to win and you try to win for them. Of course they all want to know if you are going to win the Championship. All you can tell them is that it is not impossible.

People ask me how long I will go on racing but I don't know. I have changed my plans many times in the last three or four years. All I want to do at the moment is concentrate on my job at Ferrari. I intend to spend a lot of time in Italy. It is written into my contract that I will take part in the technical discussions at the team. I want to do all I can for Ferrari. I told them in July 1989, that if they wanted to beat McLaren Honda in 1990 they had to forget '89 and look ahead to the next year right then.

DA: Ferrari were further strengthened by the signing of another defector from McLaren, designer Steve Nichols. Winter testing suggested Ferrari were narrowing the gap between themselves and McLaren. Prost and Mansell were promised more power and better reliability. Mansell was impressed with his new team-mate. He said: 'Alain is motivated like there's no tomorrow. We're working well together.'

162

The real test would begin in Pheonix on 11 March. That's where the talking would stop. Not, though, until Alain had attempted to end the feud with Senna and McLaren, a feud he believed might have tragic consequences. Alain was still haunted by the memory of Gilles Villeneuve's fatal accident in 1982. The French-Canadian felt betrayed when his partner at Ferrari, Didier Pironi, defied rank, refused to hold station and beat him to the line in the San Marino Grand Prix at Imola. Thirteen days later, in the final qualifying session for the Belgian Grand Prix at Zolder, an embittered Villeneuve ran into Jochen Mass' March and was catapulted to his death.

AP: I cannot forget what happened to Gilles. I am convinced that his state of mind had a lot to do with the accident, and there were similarities with our situation. People were talking about grudges and revenge, and that scared me. Motor racing is dangerous enough already without that sort of talk. I wanted us to be sensible and make sure no-one was hurt because of things that happened the year before. It was a new season, the chance for all of us to start again. My hope was that Ayrton, Nigel and I could concentrate on the racing and have no more problems.

DA: Alain's earnest endeavours to bury the hatchet met with a cool response at McLaren. Senna said he had no inclination to shake hands with his former team-mate and Dennis replied: 'The gesture would have had more value if he hadn't made it public.' Despite the reaction – or lack of it – Alain had made his point. Now it was time to get down to business and the 1990 Formula One World Championship.

It was not an auspicious start. Ferrari were dogged by gearbox and engine problems during practice. Both drivers complained that under braking the V12 would want to 'go on'. At the end of the first qualifying session on the downtown street circuit Prost was seventh, Mansell seventeenth. Both hoped for better fortune on the second day. Instead, it rained. Here, in the Arizona desert, of all places. Their places were unchanged as they lined up for the United States Grand Prix.

Race day was cool and cloudy, but the rain didn't return until the action was over. Not that there was a great deal of action as far as Alain was concerned. Oil pressure problems soon made it obvious that his first race for Ferrari would be short-lived. The tell-tale sign of smoke grew ever more evident as he eased his way up to fourth place. Alain could push his car no further. He slowed down on lap 23, pulled into the pits and climbed from the cockpit. Mansell was running fifth when, spectacularly, 'a big explosion in the engine' sent smoke and then flames shooting from the back of the Ferrari. The car jerked sideways but Mansell managed to control it and bring it to a standstill. Senna went on to win the race after resisting a spirited fight by young Frenchman Jean Alesi in the Pirelli-shod Tyrrell Ford.

AP: I said before the race that Pheonix would be the worst place for us, even worse than Monaco. A stop-start circuit does not suit the Ferrari V12. I was sure we would be much better on a real race track. It was good to get Pheonix out of the way. McLaren were certainly strong, we knew that. But we were confident we could improve. There was plenty of racing to be done – and that was all I wanted to do. Just race. For the pleasure.

DA: The racing brought pleasure for Alain at the new Interlagos circuit, scene of the Brazilian Grand Prix a fortnight later. The locals were preparing to celebrate another Senna triumph, but he had the door closed on him by backmarker Satoru Nakajima, in the Tyrrell Ford, and was forced to pit for repairs. Guess who was right behind to pick up the pieces? Yes, it was win No. 40 for the defending champion.

AP: They don't come much sweeter than that. Beating Senna in Sao Paulo made it a fantastic day for Ferrari, but especially for me.

For the Record: 1973-1989

1973 French Junior Karting Champion
1973 European Junior Karting Champion
1974 French Senior Karting Champion
1975 French Senior Karting Champion
Winner Pilote Elf, Renault-Elf Winfield School, Paul Ricard Circuit,
25 October

1976

Formula Renault   **Martini-Renault MK 17**

Date	Venue	Result
4 April	Le Mans-Bugatti	1 15 laps in 26 mins 44.2 secs Average speed 142.740 kph
18 April	Nogaro	1 20 laps in 28 mins 30.7 secs Average speed 131.314 kph Pole position; fastest lap
1 May	Magny-Cours	1 20 laps in 30 mins 49.5 secs Average speed 147.776 kph Pole position; fastest lap
23 May	Charade	1 10 laps in 33 mins 56.8 secs Average speed 143.839 kph Pole position; fastest lap

Date	*Venue*	*Result*
20 June	Folembray	1 35 laps in 33 mins 57.3 secs Average speed 125.734 kph Pole position
27 June	Rouen	1 15 laps in 31 mins 36.6 secs Average speed 155.820 kph Fastest lap
4 July	Paul Ricard	1 15 laps in 32 mins 49.7 secs Average speed 159.283 kph Fastest lap
11 July	Magny-Cours	1 20 laps in 31 mins 35.7 secs Average speed 144.174 kph Pole position; fastest lap
5 September	Dijon	1 20 laps in 24 mins 14.2 secs Average speed 162.844 kph Pole position; fastest lap
19 September	Nogaro	1 20 laps in 27 mins 59.6 secs Average speed 133.746 kph Fastest lap
30 September	Albi	1 20 laps in 26 mins 32.6 secs Average speed 164.378 kph Fastest lap
17 October	Paul Ricard	1 20 laps in 28 mins 04.1 secs Average speed 139.523 kph Fastest lap
24 October	Imola	Did not finish (fuel feed) Fastest lap

1976 Formula Renault French Champion

Formula Renault Europe   Lola-Renault

Date	Venue	Result
9 May	Dijon	Did not finish (fuel leak) Won eliminator Heat 2 and qualified in pole position for final ahead of Heat 1 winner Didier Pironi
16 May	Zolder	Did not finish (spun out)
Date	*Venue*	*Result*

1977

Formula Renault Europe   Martini-Renault MK 20

Date	Venue	Result
27 March	Le Mans-Bugatti	3
11 April	Nogaro	1 25 laps in 33 mins 21.4 secs Average speed 140.301 kph Fastest lap
17 April	Hockenheim	5
1 May	Magny-Cours	1 25 laps in 37 mins 18.5 secs Average speed 152.620 kph
22 May	Monaco	2 Fastest lap
29 May	Pau	2 Fastest lap
5 June	Zolder	Did not finish (engine) Pole position
19 June	Charade	3
26 June	Rouen	1 20 laps in 40 mins 21.8 secs Average speed 164.793 kph Pole position; fastest lap
3 July	Dijon	13

Life in the fast lane

Date	Venue	Results
10 July	Nogaro	1 25 laps in 34 mins 02.1 secs Average speed 137.505 kph Pole position
17 July	Magny-Cours	Did not finish (gearbox) Pole position
24 July	Paul Ricard	5
11 September	Monza	1 20 laps in 39 mins 40.5 secs Average speed 175.424 kph Fastest lap
25 September	Albi	1 25 laps in 31 mins 48.1 secs Average speed 171.499 kph Fastest lap
15 October	Paul Ricard	7 Fastest lap

1977 Champion Formula Renault Europe

Formula 2 **Kauhsen-Renault**

Date	Venue	Result
10 July	Nogaro	10
2 October	Estoril	Did not finish (lost wheel)

1978

Formula Three **Martini-Renault MK 21B**

Date	Venue	Result
23 April	Zolder	10
7 May	Monaco	4
28 May	Nürburgring	Did not finish (engine)

Date	Venue	Result
4 June	Dijon	10
25 June	Monza	14
2 July	Paul Ricard	3
16 July	Magny-Cours	Did not finish (engine)
26 August	Donington	6
29 July	Silverstone	3
15 September	Jarama	1 30 laps in 44 mins 02.54 secs Average speed 139.141 kph Pole position; fastest lap
8 October	Vallelunga	Did not finish (engine)

1978 French Formula Three Champion
1978 European Formula Three Championship: Ninth

Formula Two — Chevron-Hart

Date	Venue	Result
15 May	Pau	Did not finish (engine)

1979

Formula Three — Martini-Renault MK 27

Date	Venue	Result
18 March	Vallelunga	2 Fastest lap
16 April	Österreichring	1 45 mins 39.7 secs at 187.404 kph
23 April	Zolder	1 33 mins 33.18 secs at 159.191 kph

Life in the fast lane

Date	Venue	Result
1 May	Magny-Cours	1 37 mins 22.6 secs at 154.1 kph Fastest lap
20 May	Donington	3
26 May	Monaco	1 39 mins 08.32 secs at 121.856 kph Pole position; fastest lap
4 June	Zandvoort	1 38 mins 08.453 secs at 168.055 kph Pole position; fastest lap
24 June	Monza	Did not finish (half-shaft)
5 August	Knutstorp	1 47 mins 05.29 secs at 128.9 kph Pole position; fastest lap
12 August	Mantorp Park	Did not finish (engine) Pole position
9 September	Jarama	1 44 mins 07.93 secs at 138.857 kph Pole position; fastest lap
15 September	La Châtre	1 Fastest lap
22 September	Albi	1 Fastest lap

1979 European Formula Three Champion
1979 French Formula Three Champion
Winner Renault R5 Endurance Race

1980

Formula One   McLaren-Ford

Date	Venue	Grid position	Result
13 January	Argentina	12	6
27 January	Brazil	13	5
1 March	South Africa	n/a	Did not start (spun out during qualifying, after broken suspension, fractured wrist)
30 March	Long Beach USA	n/a	Did not start
4 May	Belgium	19	Did not finish
18 May	Monaco	10	Did not finish
29 June	France	7	Did not finish
13 July	Great Britain	7	6
10 August	West Germany	14	11
17 August	Austria	12	7
31 August	Netherlands	18	6
14 September	Italy	24	7
28 September	Canada	12	Did not finish
4 October	Watkins Glen USA	13	Did not start (spun out due to mechanical failure)

1980 Formula One World Championship: Fifteenth (5 points)
Competed in Renault 5 non-championship event to celebrate anniversary of Magny-Cours circuit

1981

Formula One   Renault Turbo

Date	Venue	Grid position	Result
15 March	Long Beach USA	14	Did not finish
29 March	Brazil	5	Did not finish
12 April	Argentina	2	3
3 May	San Marino	4	Did not finish

Life in the fast lane

Date	Venue	Grid position	Result
17 May	Belgium	12	Did not finish
31 May	Monaco	9	Did not finish
21 June	Spain	5	Did not finish
5 July	France		1 1 hr 35 mins 48.13 secs Average speed 190.392 kph Fastest lap
18 July	Great Britain	2	Did not finish
2 August	West Germany	Pole	2
16 August	Austria	2	Did not finish
29 August	Netherlands	Pole	1 1 hr 40 mins 22.43 secs Average speed 183.014 kph
13 September	Italy	3	1 1 hr 26 mins 33.89 secs Average speed 209.045 kph
27 September	Canada	5	Not ranked
17 October	Las Vegas USA	5	2

1981 Formula One World Championship: Fifth (43 points)

1982

Formula One   Renault Turbo

Date	Venue	Grid position	Result
23 January	South Africa	5	1 1 hr 32 mins 08.401 secs Average speed 205.779 kph Fastest lap
21 March	Brazil	Pole	1 1 hr 44 mins 33.134 secs Average speed 181.892 kph Fastest lap

Date	Venue	Grid position	Result
4 April	Long Beach USA	4	Did not finish
25 April	San Marino	2	Did not finish
9 May	Belgium	Pole	Did not finish
23 May	Monaco	4	Did not finish Ranked 7
6 June	Detroit USA	Pole	Not ranked Fastest lap
13 June	Canada	3	Did not finish
3 July	Netherlands	2	Did not finish
18 July	Great Britain	8	6
25 July	France	2	2
8 August	West Germany	2	Did not finish
15 August	Austria	3	Did not finish
29 August	Switzerland	Pole	2 Fastest lap
12 September	Italy	5	Did not finish
25 September	Las Vegas USA	Pole	4

1982 Formula One World Championship: Fourth (34 points)

Rallying	**Renault 5 Turbo** Co-driver Jean-Marc Andrié	
Date	*Venue*	*Result*
October	Rallye du Var	Did not finish (spun out, accelerator cable jammed)

Formula Pacific   Ralt RT 4

Date	Venue	Grid position	Result
November	Calder, Australia Formula Pacific Grand Prix	Pole	1 1 hr 07 mins 18.65 sec Average speed 160.44 kph

1983

Formula One   Renault Turbo

Date	Venue	Grid position	Result
13 March	Brazil	2	7
27 March	Long Beach USA	8	11
17 April	France	Pole	1 1 hr 34 mins 13.913 secs Average speed 199.767 kph Fastest lap
1 May	San Marino	4	2
15 May	Monaco	Pole	3
22 May	Belgium	Pole	1 1 hr 27 mins 11.502 secs Average speed 191.729 kph
5 June	Detroit USA	13	8
12 June	Canada	2	5
16 July	Great Britain	3	1 1 hr 24 mins 39.78 secs Average speed 224.069 kph Fastest lap
7 August	West Germany	5	4
14 August	Austria	5	1 1 hr 24 mins 32.745 secs Average speed 223.495 kph Fastest lap
28 August	Netherlands	4	Did not finish
11 September	Italy	5	Did not finish
25 September	Brands Hatch European Grand Prix	8	2
15 October	South Africa	5	Did not finish

1983 Formula One World Championship: Second (57 points)

1984

Formula One   **McLaren-TAG-Porsche Turbo**

Date	Venue	Grid position	Result
25 March	Brazil	4	1 1 hr 42 mins 34.392 secs Average speed 179.511 kph Fastest lap
7 April	South Africa	5	2
29 April	Belgium	8	Did not finish
6 May	San Marino	2	1 1 hr 36 mins 5.679 secs Average speed 187.254 kph
20 May	France	2	7 Fastest lap
3 June	Monaco	Pole	1 1 hr 01 mins 07.74 secs Average speed 100.775 kph
17 June	Canada	2	3
24 June	Detroit USA	2	4
8 July	Dallas USA	7	Did not finish
22 July	Great Britain	2	Did not finish
5 August	West Germany	Pole	1 1 hr 24 mins 43.21 secs Average speed 211.803 kph Fastest lap
19 August	Austria	2	Did not finish
26 August	Netherlands	Pole	1 1 hr 37 mins 21.468 secs Average speed 186.050 kph
9 September	Italy	2	Did not finish

Date	Venue	Grid position	Result
7 October	Nürburgring European Grand Prix	2	1 1 hr 35 mins 13.284 secs Average speed 191.751 kph
21 October	Portugal	2	1 1 hr 41 mins 11.753 secs Average speed 180.540 kph

1984 Formula One World Championship: Second (71.5 points)

1985

Formula One   McLaren-TAG-Porsche Turbo

Date	Venue	Grid position	Result
7 April	Brazil	6	1 1 hr 41 mins 26.115 secs Average speed 181.527 kph Fastest lap
21 April	Portugal	2	Did not finish
5 May	San Marino	6	Disqualified (won race but car infringed weight regulations)
19 May	Monaco	5	1 1 hr 51 mins. 58.034 secs Average speed 138.434 kph
16 June	Canada	5	3
23 June	Detroit USA	4	Did not finish
7 July	France	4	3

Date	Venue	Grid position	Result
21 July	Great Britain	3	1 1 hr 18 mins 10.436 secs Average speed 235.375 kph Fastest lap
4 August	West Germany	3	2
18 August	Austria	Pole	1 1 hr 20 mins 12.583 secs Average speed 231.132 kph Fastest lap
25 August	Netherlands	3	2 Fastest lap
8 September	Italy	5	1 1 hr 17 mins 59.451 secs Average speed 227.565 kph
15 September	Belgium	Pole	3 Fastest lap
6 October	Brands Hatch	6	4
19 October	South Africa	9	3
3 November	Australia	4	Did not finish

1985 Formula One World Champion (73 points)

1986

Formula One			**McLaren-TAG-Porsche Turbo**
Date	*Venue*	*Grid position*	*Result*
23 March	Brazil	9	Did not finish
13 April	Spain	4	3

Date	Venue	Grid position	Result
27 April	San Marino	4	1 1 hr 32 mins 28.408 secs Average speed 196.208 kph
11 May	Monaco	Pole	1 1 hr 55 mins 41.060 secs Average speed 134.634 kph Fastest lap
25 May	Belgium	3	6 Fastest lap
15 June	Canada	4	2
22 June	Detroit USA	7	3
6 July	France	5	2
13 July	Great Britain	6	3
27 July	West Germany	2	6
10 August	Hungary	3	Did not finish
17 August	Austria	5	1 1 hr 21 mins 22.531 secs Average speed 227.821 kph
7 September	Italy	2	Disqualified (infringed start regulations)
21 September	Portugal	3	2
12 October	Mexico	6	2
26 October	Australia	4	1 1 hr 54 mins 20.388 secs Average speed 162.609 kph

1986 Formula One World Champion (72 points)

1987

Formula One			McLaren-TAG-Porsche

Date	Venue	Grid position	Result
12 April	Brazil	5	1 1 hr 39 mins 45.141 secs Average speed 184.592 kph
3 May	San Marino	4	Did not finish
17 May	Belgium	6	1 1 hr 27 mins 93.217 secs Average speed 205.680 kph Fastest lap
31 May	Monaco	4	Did not finish (but ranked 9)
21 June	Detroit USA	5	3
5 July	France	2	3
12 July	Great Britain	4	Did not finish
26 July	West Germany	3	Did not finish (but ranked 7)
9 August	Hungary	4	3
16 August	Austria	9	6
6 September	Italy	5	15
20 September	Portugal	3	1 1 hr 37 mins 03.906 secs Average speed 188.224 kph
27 September	Spain	7	2
18 October	Mexico	5	Did not finish
1 November	Japan	2	7 Fastest lap
15 November	Australia	2	Did not finish

1987 Formula One World Championship: Fourth (46 points)

1988

Formula One			McLaren-Honda Turbo
Date	*Venue*	*Grid position*	*Result*
3 April	Brazil	3	1 1 hr 36 mins 06.857 secs Average speed 188.438 kph
1 May	San Marino	2	2 Fastest lap
15 May	Monaco	2	1 1 hr 57 mins 17.077 secs Average speed 132.797 kph
29 May	Mexico	2	1 1 hr 30 mins 15.737 secs Average speed 196.898 kph Fastest lap
12 June	Canada	2	2
19 June	Detroit USA	4	2 Fastest lap
3 July	France	Pole	1 1 hr 37 mins 37.328 secs Average speed 187.482 kph Fastest lap
10 July	Great Britain	4	Did not finish
24 July	West Germany	2	2
7 August	Hungary	7	2 Fastest lap
28 August	Belgium	2	2
11 September	Italy	2	Did not finish
25 September	Portugal	Pole	1 1 hr 37 mins 40.958 secs Average speed 187.034 kph

Date	Venue	Grid position	Result
2 October	Spain	2	1 1 hr 48 mins 43.851 secs Average speed 167.586 kph Fastest lap
30 October	Japan	2	2
13 November	Australia	2	1 1 hr 53 mins 14.676 secs Average speed 164.225 kph Fastest lap

1988 Formula One World Championship: Second (87 points)

1989

Formula One			McLaren-Honda V10
Date	*Venue*	*Grid position*	*Result*
26 March	Brazil	6	2 1 hr 39 mins 06.553 secs Average speed 185.790 kph
23 April	San Marino	2	2 1 hr 27 mins 31.470 secs Average speed 200.392 kph Fastest lap
7 May	Monaco	1	2 1 hr 53 mins 25.780 secs Average speed 134.365 kph Fastest lap
28 May	Mexico	1	5 1 hr 36 mins 17.544 secs Average speed 190.077 kph

Date	Venue	Grid position	Result
4 June	Phoenix, USA	1	1 2 hrs 1 min 33.133 secs Average speed 140.608 kph
18 June	Canada	1	Did not finish
9 July	France	2	1 1 hr 38 mins 29.411 secs Average speed 185.830 kph
16 July	Great Britain	1	1 1 hr 19 mins 22.131 secs Average speed 231.253 kph
30 July	West Germany	2	2 1 hr 22 mins 01.453 secs Average speed 223.738 kph
13 August	Hungary	5	4 1 hr 50 mins 22.827 secs Average speed 166.082 kph
27 August	Belgium	1	2 1 hr 40 mins 55.500 secs Average speed 181.537 kph Fastest lap
10 September	Italy	4	1 1 hr 19 mins 27.550 secs Average speed 232.119 kph Fastest lap
24 September	Portugal	3	2 1 hr 37 mins 21.183 secs Average speed 190.348 kph
1 October	Spain	4	3 1 hr 48 mins 42.055 secs Average speed 169.960 kph

Date	Venue	Grid position	Result
22 October	Japan	1	Did not finish
5 November	Australia	2	Did not start

1989 Formula One World Champion (76 points)

Postscript

As of the 1990 Brazilian Grand Prix, Alain Prost has won forty Grand Prix races. He holds the record for the absolute number of championship victories since Formula One started in 1950. The previous record holder was Jackie Stewart, with twenty-seven wins ending in 1973. Prost equalled Stewart's record on 17 May 1987 by winning the Belgian Grand Prix.

Index

Adelaide, 97, 98, 111, 113, 121, 150, *152*,
    153
Alazar Trophy, 21
Alboreto, Michele, 56, 74, 84–94 *passim.*, *95*,
    96, 122
Alesi, Jean, 164
Alliot, Philippe, *138*, 143
Almirante Brown, 40
America, Latin 82 *see also individual countries*
    and under Grand Prix
America, North, 37, 38 *see also* Canada *and,*
    under Grand Prix, Canadian, US, US
    West
Argentina, 118
Arnoux, René, *45*, 47, *47*, *51*, 52, *55*, 56–8,
    61, 106, 134, 140, 157
Arrows, 10
Australia, 97, 111, 150, 161
Austria, 77, 90, 109, 121, 125
Automobile Club of Hungary, 106
Automobile Club of Monaco, 77
Auxemery, Jannick, 19

BMW, 65
Bakalian, Bernard, 7
Barnard, John, 46, 65, 71, 83, *83*, 102, 103
Belgium, 29, 93, 104, 122, 151
Benetton, 104, 111, 156, 159, 161
Berger, Gerhard, 104, 111, 126, 131, 140,
    143, 147, 156, 159, 160
Bernard, John, 159
Bhat, Erik, 37
Bosch, 70
Bousquet, Jean-Louis, 17, 20, 29, 30, 31, *31*
Boutsen, Thierry, 120, 158, 161
Brabham, 37, 40, 50, 53, 54, 60, 116
Brabham BMW, 62, 63, 87
Brands Hatch, 61, 73, 82, 93, *93*, 94, *95*, 97,
    98, 102, 106, *107*, 108
    Clearways, 95
    Paddock Bend, *107*
Brazil 14, 41, 55, *55*, 74, 75, 77, 86, 99, 100,

117, 118, *119*, 121, 132, 146, 156
Brundle, Martin, 95, 161
Brussel, Jacques, 29
Budapest, 106, 140
Buenos Aires, 40, 82

Canada, 37, 75
Capelli, Ivan, 44, *149*
Castaing, François, 32
Chabot, Jeanne, 25
Champion of Champions Trophy, 134, *134*
Champs Elysées, 98
Cheever, Eddie, 20, 21, 59, 66
Chevron-Hart, 33
Clark, Jim, 121, 153
Cogan, Teddy, 38
Coulon, Jacques, 30
Cudini, Alain, 29

Dallas, 75–6
Dallest, Richard, 29, *31*, 36
Dalmas, Yannick, 143
Daly, Derek, 43
Danielson team, *28*, 29
De Angelis, Elio, 40, 54, 56, 77, 85, *85*, 86,
    87, 90, 94, 95, 105, 116
De Cesaris, Andrea, 65, 88, 148, 157
de Chaunac, Hughes, 32, 33, 34
de Lautour, Simon, 22, 23, 25
Denisot, Michel, 14
Denmark, 117
Dennis, Ron, 9, 48, 64–5, 67, 68, 71, 86, 89,
    91, 95, 101, 102, 108, 112, 114, 116,
    120, 124, 129, 134, 136, *136*, 146, 148–
    50, *155*, 156, 157, 159, 163
Depailler, Patrick, *45*, 46
Descombes, Robert, 34
Detroit, 87, 104
Dijon, 29, 50, *51*, 52, 76
    Pouas Curve, 76
Dudot, Bernard, 32, 66
Dungl, Andrea, 73

185

Dungl, Joseph, *72*, 73
Dungl, Willy, 71

Ecclestone, Bernie, 37, 48, 53, 76, *119*
Elf, 26, 30, 33, 34, 63
   Elf 2 – Renault, 33
   see also Renault – Elf Winfield School
England, 38, 121, 151
Estoril, 33, 78, *78*, 126, 132, 143, 144, 156
Euroburn, 140

FIA Tribunal, 55, 161
FISA, 43, 48, 54–5, 77, 129, 150
FOCA, 43, 48, 54–5, 71, *119*
Fabi, Teo, 89, 120
Fabre, Michel, 18
Fangio, Juan Manuel, 40, 91, *115*, 134, 161
Ferrari, 40, 56, 58, 61, 64, 74, 82, 84, 86,
   87, 94, 103, 108, 126, 139, 156–64
   passim
Ferrari, Enzo, 58, 117–18
Fittipaldi, Emerson, 21, 36, 40
football *see* soccer
Formula Atlantic, 38
Formula Ford, 32
Formula One *see* Grand Prix
Formula Pacific, 97
Formula Renault Europe, 27–31, *28*, 32, 33
Formula Renault French Championship, 26
Formula Three
   European Championship, 33, 34
   French Championship, 33, 34
Formula Two, 32, 33, 34, 48
Formula Vee, 32
Francorchamps *see* Spa Francorchamps

Gabbiani, Beppe, 20
Garza, Josele, 155
Germany, 32, 106, 121, 151
Ghinzani, Piercarlo, *96*
Giacomelli, Bruno, 54
Glavany, Jean, 98
Goodyear, 113
Gordini, Amédée, 73
Goto, Osamu, 144
Grand Prix
   Argentinian, 40–1, 49
   Australian, 93, 111, 112, 114, 126, 150,
     153, 161
   Austrian, 63, 89, 91, 108, 109, 124, *125*
   Belgian, 43, 58, 87, 104, 132, 141, *141*,
     142, 163
   Brazilian, 14, 42, 55, *55*, 56, 74, 75, 82,
     92, 98, 101, 103, 108, 109, 114, 116,
     117, 118, *134*, 164
   British, 65, 88, 105, *107*, 139, 140, 153,
     158

Canadian, 44, 52, 58, 87, 104
Dutch, 36, 50, 52, 60–1, 65, 69, 78, 91
European, 61, 78, 93, 94, 97
French, 50, *51*, 56, *57*, 76, 87, 106–8, 121,
   124, 134, 143
German, 50, 58, 89, 140, 158
Hungarian, 26, 106–8, 121, 140
Italian, 44, 47, 61, 78, 92, 109, 125, 126,
   142, 159
Japanese, 126, *130*, 146–50, 151
Mexican, 111, 126, 128, 157
Monaco, 77, 91, 134, 157
Portuguese, 78, 84–5, 110, *127*, 146
San Marino, 55, 76, 85, 121, 157, 163
South African, 56, 66, 93, 97, 103
Spanish, 43, 126, 145, 160
US, 37, 38, 87, 163
US West, 48
see also host countries, cities and venues
Grand Prix Drivers' Association, *119*
Grand Prix Former Drivers Club, 134, *134*
Greece, 117
Gugelmin, Mauricio, 148
Guiter, François, 30, 32, 34, 36, 63

Hanon, Bernard, 51
Hanrioud, Jean-Pierre, 67
Hart engine, 89
Head, Patrick, 99
Hill, Graham, 105
Hockenheim, 30, 46, 58, *122*
Hogan, John, 64–5
Holland, 36
Honda, 84, 100, 108, 112, 117, 118, 120,
   122, 125, 128–9, 131, 136, 140, 142,
   143, 144, 145, 148, 150, 151
Hungary, 106, 109, 134, 151
Hunt, James, 64

Ickx, Jacky, 40, 77–8
Illouz, François, 132
Imola, 26, 44, 47, 76, 85, 103–4, 121, 132,
   134, *137*, 156, 157, 163
   Tosa corner, 76
Indycars, 38, 155
Interlagos, 41–2
Italy, 26, 110, 151, 159

Jabouille, Jean-Pierre, 41, *45*, 46, 47, 153
Jacarepagua, 84
Japan, 108, 128, 147, *149*
Jarama, 33, 34, 36
Jarier, Jean-Pierre, 45
Jenkins, Alan, 71
Jerez, 106, 132, *145*, 155
Johansson, Stefan, 86, 89, 94, 95, 117, 120,
   122, 130, 145

Jones, Alan, 50, 52, 105, 116

KKK, 102
Karting, 15–21, *16, 18, 19*, 22, 23
  European championship, 20
  French championship, 20, 21
  Rive de Gier Club, 17, 18
  World championship, 18, 20
Kauhsen, 32
Kawamoto, Mr, 129
Knutstrop, 34
Kyalami, 42, 54, 67, 74, 97, 105
  Leukoop, 42
la Châtre, 34
Laffite, Jacques, 14, 41, 44, *45*, 47, *73*, 76, 81, *93*, 94, 95, 98, 104–5, 106, 112, 116, 126, 131
Landereau, 106
Larrousse, Gérard, 34, 47, *47, 51*, 52, 56, 105
Lauda, Niki, 37, 54, 56, 65, 68, 70–87 *passim., 78, 79*, 90, 92, 94, 112, 121, 153
Le Castellet, 22
Le Mans, 30
Légion d'Honneur, 98
Lesgourges, Michel, 19
Levent, Gilles, 132
Lidouren, Fernand, 34
Ligier, 40, 47, 130
Loire, 9
Long Beach, 42, 43, 48, *49*
Lorrette, 9
Lotus, 49, 64, 82, 100, 101, 108, 109, 120, 125
Lotus-Renault, 85, 99, 100, 103

McLaren, 9, 36, 37, 38, 42–9 *passim., 44*, 54, 64–71 *passim., 69*, 74–90 *passim.*, 94, 98–151 *passim., 136*, 156–63 *passim*
  M23, 65
  M24, 65
  M29, 42, 44, 65
  M29B, 42
  M29C, 42
  M30, 44, 65
  MP4, 65
  MP4/2, 68
  MP4-2B, 83
  MP4-2C, 102
  Motul M1, 64
  Project Four, 54–5
  Project Team, 64
  Project Three, 64
  Rondel Racing, 64
  Woking, 68, 108, 114, 145, 146, 147, 148
McLaren, Bruce, 64

McLaren-Honda, *130*, 131, *133*, 151, 156, 162
McLaren-TAG-Porsche, 65, 68, 70, 75, 82, 87, 102
Magny-Cours, 22, 26, 30, 32, 34, *45*
Mangé, Bernard, 26, 29
Mansell, Nigel, 88, 93, 99, 100, *100*, 103, 108–14 *passim.*, 120–1, 122, 124, 128, *128*, 129, *145*, 146, 147, 156, 162, 163, 164
March, 149, 163
Marlboro, 40, 48, 64–5, 82, 117
Marlboro-McLaren, *153*
Martini, 22, 23, *24*, 25, 26, *27*, 33
Martini-Renault, 33, 34, *36*
Martini, Tico, 32
Mass, Jochen, 163
Mayer, Teddy, 37, 38, 42, 43, 44, 48, 65
Mexico, 111, 126, 128
Mezger, Hans, 66, 102
Mitterrand, François (President), 98
Monaco, 30, 33, 34, *35*, 36, 43, 60, 84, 86, 87, 91, 104, 108, 121, 122, 134
  Saint Devôte run-off zone, 86
Moncet, Jean-Louis, 14, 37
Montreal, 87, 101, *138*, 158
Monza, 30, 52, 61, 78, 92, 125, 143, 158, 159
Morizot, Yves, 131
Murray, Gordon, 50, 53, *61*, 74, 116, 117, 120, 129

Nakajima, Satoru, 125, 140, 164
Nannini, Alessandro, 140, 161
Necchi, Piero, 20
Nichols, Steve, 71, 116, 124, *133*, 162
Nicolas, Jean-Pierre, 26
Nivelles, 18
Nogaro, 30, 33
Norway, 117
Nürburgring, 78, 89

ORECA, 32, 33
Oatley, Neil, 116, 117, 142, 147
Ojjeh, Mansour, 65, 114, 136
Opert, Fred, 77, 89, 124
Österreichring, 77, 89, 124
  Bosch Curve, 124
  Rindt Curve, 77

Paletti, Ricardo, 58
Parilla and Komet engine, 18
Paris, 145
Patrese, Riccardo, 20, 41–2, 56, 86
Pau, 30, 33, 91
Paul Ricard, 21–3, 30–1, 38, *39*, 56–8, *57*, 68–9, 87, 105

La Verrerie 'S' bend, 87, 88, 105
Pelletier, Claude, 18
Perez-Sala, Luis, 155
Pescarolo, Henri, 85
Peterson, Ronnie, 21
Peugeot, 98, 162
  Peugeot 205 Turbo, 16, 98
Philip Morris Europe, 64
Phoenix, 158, 162
Piccinini, Marco, 117–18
Pilote Elf, 12, *24*, 25, 26
Piquet, Nelson, 37, 49, 50, *51*, 52, 55, 56,
  60–1, *62*, 63, 76, 77, 86, 87, 99, *100*,
  103, 108–13 *passim.*, 120–1, 122, 124,
  125, 129, 131, 143, 157
Pirelli, 111
Pironi, Didier, 29, 30, *45*, 54, 56, *57*, 58, 163
Pirro, Emanuele, 130, *130*
Pope, the, 97
Porsche, 65, 70, 84, 101, 102, 117, 122
Portugal, 110, 126, 143, 147, 160
Prost, André (father), 10, 15, 16, *75*, *154*,
  155
Prost, Anne-Marie (wife), 19–20, 45, 46, 53,
  61, 68, 81, *81*, 91, 97, 111, 112, 113,
  118, 131
Prost, Daniel (brother), 10, 11, 110–11
Prost, Marie-Rose (mother), 10, 13, 14, *75*
Prost, Nicolas (son), 52, 53, 61, 81, *81*

Rafaelli, Antoine, 22, 23, 25
Ragnotti, Jean, 29, 47
Rainier, Prince of Monaco, 91
Ramirez, Jo, *134*, 143
Renault, 26, 32, 34, 40, 47–71 *passim.*, *47*,
  62, 74, 84, 101, 106, 108, 156, 162
  Boulogne-Billancourt, 66
  Renault 20TS four-cylinder, 32
  Renault RE-, 40 *60*
  Reanult Turbo, 47, *49*, 52, 153
  Renix, 66
  V6-Renault Sport engine, 33
  Viry-Chatillon, 59, 66
  see also Formula Renault
Renault-Elf Winfield School, 21–3
Renault Sport, 32, 34, 47, 59, 66, 106
Reutemann, Carlos, 49, 52
Rio (de Janeiro), 14, 82, 84, 99, 100, 102,
  103, 121, 132
Rives, Johnny, 14, 67, 73, 106
Rome, 97
Rosberg, Keke, 55, 56, *56*, 84–95 *passim.*,
  102, 103, 104, *107*, 109–17 *passim.*, 132
Rouen, 30

SOVAME, 18
Sage, Jean, 106–8
Saint Chamond, 9, 10, 14, 17, 19, 22, 46,
  52, 58, 61, 98, 118, 143
Salon de l'Automobile, 144
San Marino, 157, 163
Sao Paulo, 164
Scandinavia, 82
Scheckter, Jody, 41, 76
Schlesser, Jean-Louis, 142
Senna, Ayrton, 77, 85, 86, 88–9, 90, 93, 99,
  100–1, *100*, 103, 104, 108, 110, 111,
  117, 120–1, 122–4, 125, *130*, 131, 132,
  133, *133*, 136, 138, 140–2, *141*, 143–4,
  145–51 *passim.*, *149*, 156–164 *passim*
Sestriere, 103, 113
Shell, 150, 151
Silverstone, 33, 88, 143, 153, 158
Snobeck, Danny, 29, 30, *31*
soccer, 12–14, *11*, *12*, *13*
Sourd, Marc, 29
South Africa, 53, 54, *54*, 56, *62*, 63, 74–5
Spa-Francorchamps, 87, 93, 94, 122, 126
Spain, 49, 103, 144, 145–6
Squale and Python chassis, 18
Stewart, Jackie, *7*, 121, 122, *125*, 126, *127*
Suzuka, 130, *130*, 146, 160
Sweden, 117
Switzerland, resident of, 68, 143

TAG, 65, 117
Tambay, Patrick, 23, 38, 56, 64, 76, 116
Todt, Jean, 98
Toivonen, Henri, 20
Tokyo, 150
Toleman, 77, 89
Trundle, Neil, 64
Turkey, 117
Tyrrell, 43, 64
Tyrrell Ford, 164

United Kingdom, 32, 91

Vacquand chassis, 17
Villeneuve, Gilles, 54, 58, 76, 163

Warwick, Derek, 74, 76, 100
Watkins Glen, 37, 44
Watson, John, 38, 42, 46, *51*, 52, 56, 65, 94
Williams, 40, 50, 76, 84, 92, 99, 100, 101,
  103, 108, 111, 112, 116, 120, 125, 156,
  159
Williams, Frank, 99–100
Williams-Honda, 87, 99, 103, 121, 128
Williams-Renault, 158

World Championship (Formula One), 59, 77, 80, *107*, *149*
Wright, Tim, 71, 109, *110*, 116, 147

Yens, 68

Zandvoort, 34, 36, 37, 50, 52, 60–1, 91–2
    Tarzan Corner, 50
Zeltweg, 34, 89, 109
Zolder, 29, 30, 34, 58, 75, 163
Zunino, Ricardo, 37
Zurini, Manon, 89